STOP
BEING

Niggardly

COAUTHORED BY KAREN HUNTER

Let's Talk About Pep by Sandy (Pep) Denton

Don't Blame It on Rio by Jewel Woods

Raising Kanye by Donda West

Pimpology by Ken Ivy

Confessions of a Video Vixen by Karrine Steffans

On the Up and Up by Brenda Stone Browder

The Wendy Williams Experience by Wendy Williams

On the Down Low by J. L. King

Wendy's Got the Heat by Wendy Williams

Al on America by the Reverend Al Sharpton

Revelations by Mason Betha

Grown-A$$ Man by Cedric the Entertainer

Ladies First by Queen Latifah

I Make My Own Rules by LL Cool J

STOP
BEING
Niggardly

And Nine Other Things Black People
Need to Stop Doing
(featuring Nannie Helen Burroughs's
Twelve Things the Negro Must Do)

KAREN HUNTER

Gallery Books   Karen Hunter Publishing

NEW YORK   LONDON   TORONTO   SYDNEY

To all who love truth, who have vision,
and who tackle life fearlessly

G
Gallery Books
A Division of Simon & Schuster, Inc.
1230 Avenue of the Americas
New York, NY 10020

Karen Hunter Publishing
A Division of Suitt-Hunter Enterprises, LLC
598 Broadway, 3rd Floor
New York, NY 10012

First Karen Hunter Publishing trade paperback edition April 2010

For information about special discounts for bulk purchases,
please contact Simon & Schuster Special Sales at 1-866-506-1949
or business@simonandschuster.com.

The Simon & Schuster Speakers Bureau can bring authors to your live event.
For more information or to book an event contact the Simon & Schuster Speakers Bureau
at 1-866-248-3049 or visit our website at www.simonspeakers.com.

Designed by Ruth Lee-Mui

Manufactured in the United States of America

1 3 5 7 9 10 8 6 4 2

Library of Congress Cataloging-in-Publication Data is available.

ISBN 978-1-4165-6374-7
ISBN 978-1-4391-2370-6 (ebook)

But seek ye first the kingdom of God, and his righteousness; and all these things shall be added unto you.

—MATTHEW 6:33

WHEN I WROTE my first book, *I Make My Own Rules* with LL Cool J in 1996, I had all of these people that I wanted to thank. I soon realized (and was told) that collaborators don't generally get to thank anyone. I have coauthored eighteen books and never had an opportunity to thank all of the people who have helped me become the writer I am, the teacher I am, the student I am, the person I am.

I want to first acknowledge God publicly. In the words of Nannie Helen Burroughs, I am putting first things first.

To my parents, Marge and Donald Hunter—both very different people, who somehow came together to provide me with the best foundation and allowed me the freedom of expression to explore all possibilities—I love you dearly.

To my brother, Kevin, thank you for forcing me to set a good example and for reminding me of where I've been, which has allowed me to continue to go where I'm going.

In my career, I've had several mentors. To Michael Goodwin, who plucked me from obscurity and gave me a vision that I, at first, could not see. Thank you for believing in me when I had doubts about myself. Thank you for sticking by me when others wouldn't. But more than that, thank you for teaching me that a constant drip of water on any hard surface will eventually wear through. You are one of the most fair-minded people I have ever known, and I appreciate you to the nth degree.

To Jennifer Raab, who treated me to lunch at the Four Seasons those many moons ago and asked me to give more of myself to help lead this next generation, thank you for giving me that wonderful gift. Teaching at Hunter College—more than anything else I've done to date—has been the reward. There is nothing that can replace the feeling of when the light bulb turns on for a student. Teaching is much more than a job and I thank you for giving me a platform to have a greater purpose.

To Hap Hairston (posthumously), I am glad that I had the opportunity to thank you many times in life.

To Teddy Van (posthumously), you had perhaps the most profound impact on me as a writer. You were truly one of the greatest minds I have ever known and you left this earth much too soon. You are missed. You are missed. You are missed.

To Louise Burke, publisher of Pocket Books (and probably many more imprints by the time this book comes out), you are the model. Thank you for giving me the opportunity to see this vision through and thank you for lending me your many years of wisdom. But more than that, thank you for being straight up and real with me from the very beginning. There are very few people who are as genuine as you are and my only hope is to be as strong a publisher and a person someday as you are. I truly thank you.

To Team Pocket Books at Simon & Schuster—Jean Ann Rose, Anthony Ziccardi, Sarah Reidy, Emilia Pisani, Keri Loyd, Melissa Gramstad, Stephen Fallert, Felice Javitz, and last but definitely not least Brigitte Smith, without whom none of this could get done—thank you for sharing your expertise, your advice and excellence in helping Karen Hunter Publishing and Karen Hunter, the person, succeed in this business. Thank you all!

To Clarence Haynes, my editor, you definitely forced me to think even more out of the box and flesh out my thoughts in a way that strengthened the book. I appreciated the back-and-forth, which gave me the balance to say what I had to say in a way that more instructive and caring. You are brilliant!

Tremell McKenzie, my sister from another mister, I want to thank you for always bringing me back to the top of the page and reminding me that as long as I put Christ first, I can have and be all things. Thank you for keeping me grounded and plugged into the Word, and encouraging and inspiring me through both your words and deeds.

To Team Poopsie: Marla Andrews and Amber Andrews. Marla, thank you for pushing the "argument," and keeping me on my toes politically. To Amber, thank you for just being one of the few truly unconditionally supportive people in my life. You guys are always there for me. And I love you!

To my support crew: Carol Mackey, Rajen Persaud, LaJoyce Brookshire, Richard Sullivan, Zondra Hughes, Karyn Grice, Vana Phillips, Supreme Master, Tracy Sherrod, Janet Hill, Jason Wright, Norwood Young, and Nicole Duncan Smith—thank you for praying for me, fasting with me, keeping me in check, believing in me, advising me, giving me insight, wisdom and love! Thank you and I love you.

And to all of my fellow writers (there are too many to name), thank you for continuing to raise the bar, and producing the work that entertain us and make us think. I know you know this, but the work you do is important. You help shape society. I want thank the ones who have come before me, my contemporaries and the ones to come.

Keep writing!

CONTENTS

Twelve Things the Negro Must Do

by Nannie Helen Burroughs

(with commentary by Karen Hunter)

Wake Up, People. Wake Up!

THERE MAY BE a black man in the Oval Office, but the journey toward true success for black people in America is far from over.

In the summer of 2009, Henry Louis (Skip) Gates Jr., a noted Harvard professor and historian, was arrested, fingerprinted, and booked. His crime? Being on his porch while black. The reports will tell you that police knew who he was when they ordered backup (for this unarmed, fifty-eight-year-old, diminutive man who walks with a cane). They knew who he was and that it was his house when they asked him to step onto his porch (because they couldn't arrest him inside his home without a warrant).

Gates was charged with disorderly conduct (charges that were later dropped) for allegedly yelling at the officers and saying something about one of their mamas. But the question still remains: if Skip Gates were a white Harvard professor returning home from China who had to push into his home because his door was stuck and police arrived, would he have been arrested, fingerprinted, and booked?

The controversial event even dragged President Barack Obama, who said that the police acted "stupidly," into the fray. The president of the United States of America was called a racist for understanding the nuances of race and knowing that profiling and racism or prejudice can so often be talked away and called something else. But those of us who have experienced it, know it when we see it. Just as there has never been an unarmed white man shot eleven, thirty-eight, or fifty times in America, had Gates been white, we would never have heard this story because it would have gone something like this:

Officer: "Oh, so sorry, sir, we had a report and had to follow up. You have a nice night now."

The president called it a "teachable moment." I call Gates-gate a moment of truth.

Truth No. 1: There is still a stigma attached to being black in America.

Truth No. 2: There is nothing that we can do about it. No matter how wealthy, how cultured, how educated, how well-spoken, you may be, if you're black, it doesn't matter—you may still be treated like a nigger.

It didn't matter in 1953 when Dorothy Dandridge (who was the first black woman nominated for a Best Actress Academy Award and the first to appear on the cover of *Life*), who was performing at an upscale hotel in Las Vegas, threatened to take a dip in their pool and they drained the pool to keep her from swimming in it.

It didn't matter in 2009, when a suburban Philadelphia pool revoked the swimming privileges (which were paid for) of a group of black and Hispanic day-care children because, as the swim-club director said in interviews, the youngsters changed the "complexion" and the "atmosphere" of the pool.

It didn't matter in 1958, when Mildred Delores Jeter, a black woman, wanted to marry her love, Richard Perry Loving, a white man. The two had to go to Washington, D.C., leaving their hometown in Virginia, which banned marriages between any person of color and any nonwhite person under something called The Racial Integrity Act.

After returning to Virginia, police raided the Lovings' home in the middle of the night, arrested them, and charged them with the criminal offense of miscegenation—a felony punishable by a prison sentence of between one and five years. This case was fought for almost twenty years, making it all the way to the Supreme Court where it was unanimously ruled in *Loving v. Virginia* (1967) that the races could indeed mix and marry.

But that didn't matter in 2009 when Keith Bardwell, a Louisiana justice of the peace, refused to marry a black man and a white woman, saying, "I just don't believe in mixing the races that way."

Despite the law and the governor calling for his resignation, Bardwell stood behind his position.

We have still not overcome.

But here comes Truth No. 3: So what to Truths 1 and 2.

It's time we focus on our lives and use the obstacles as stepping-stones. It's time we tighten our collective game and make racism and prejudice irrelevant to us the way so many other groups have done, because the real truth is, we, as black people, spend far too much time trying to get white people (and others) to accept us.

We want to live in their neighborhoods (hey there, Skip Gates), attend their schools, become members of their clubs, and go essentially where we aren't wanted. While we have every right to do so, and we should have the right (my dad was arrested helping to integrate South Carolina and Georgia, so I get that), we do so to the detriment of our own community.

While people like Gates move into "white" neighborhoods—where his neighbor called the police on him in the first place and not one of them stood up and said, "Hey, wait a minute, officers, that's Skip Gates, he's our neighbor, he lives there!"—black neighborhoods are crumbling and are full of crime, poverty, and desolation.

Wouldn't it be cool to have a professor, a doctor, a lawyer, a principal, a businessperson, all living in the so-called hood? Wouldn't that change the "complexion" dramatically and give those people—particularly the young—a great example of what to strive for?

While blacks run to "white" schools, historically black colleges, which were started when we had no options, are going out of business. Now some would say that perhaps we should let those schools close. Why do we still need black schools and black neighborhoods and black businesses? And I would love to say we don't. But the truth is, "white" colleges and teachers aren't preparing our children for the real world. They aren't teaching our children who they are. They aren't challenging them to strive for more. They aren't raising the bar on them.

"White" neighborhoods don't always welcome us and give us the community feel we deserve, and "white" businesses don't necessarily employ us and give us opportunities to prosper. During Jim Crow, black business and ownership and community thrived. We even had a hotel in Harlem where Fidel Castro and many other dignitaries stayed.

We are at a turning point in our history. We have a black president, and America will over the next three decades become a nation of "minorities," or rather, a nation where whites will be in the minority.

At the same time, blacks lag behind every other group in just about every category. We own fewer homes, own fewer businesses, have the highest dropout rates, the lowest reading scores; we lead the nation in every health-risk category from cancer and diabetes to HIV and infant mortality.

While we certainly have so many more opportunities, we have so much more work to do, and if we don't roll up our sleeves and do it now, we may never will. Because what is also happening is that fear is setting in. I predict that race-related incidents will increase over the next few years, as white men fear that their power base has dissipated.

I'm not worried about that. What I am concerned about is, how prepared are we?

In June 2009, the U.S. Supreme Court ruled in a five-to-four decision that white firefighters in New Haven, Connecticut, were unfairly denied promotions because of their race. There was a test given to 118 candidates seeking promotion to captain or lieutenant. Twenty-seven blacks were among the eligible candidates. Not one—not a single one—scored high enough to qualify for the fifteen available positions.

Instead of saying, "Oh, well, too bad, I guess we won't have any black captains or lieutenants this year," the city threw out the test and promoted nine blacks. The city was sued by twenty white (one of whom is described as white and Hispanic, whatever that is) firefighters who all passed the test yet were denied a promotion. The Supreme Court ruled in their favor, overturning a decision by a lower court.

For the record, I am all for affirmative action. Had it not been for affirmative action, my black behind would never have made it into the *Daily News,* the first major newspaper ever to lose a discrimination lawsuit. That slot as a sportswriter where I began my career was slated for a "minority." I fit the bill.

But what I clearly understood then and now (which these black firefighters and the city of New Haven, Connecticut, apparently don't) is that if I'm going to take a position set aside for a "minority," I better well be qualified for that position.

I was so paranoid about being good enough that I kept books on writing in my desk, consulted veteran writers and editors at the *News,* and had them check my work before I submitted it. I continued to work on and hone my skills. Being black may have got me in the door, but it wouldn't keep me there.

We can't whine and complain about racism when we don't step up and pass the test and make the grade.

"Boo-hoo, the test is biased," some may say. "Waaah, waaah, they have uncles and fathers and friends who are firefighters who can help them pass."

So what! Since when have black people worried about the deck being stacked against us? Since when has it not been?

That never stopped George Washington Carver, Booker T. Washington, W. E. B. Du Bois (who had to start all over again when he entered Harvard, despite having an undergraduate degree). And it didn't stop Nannie Helen Burroughs.

The test is biased? Give me a break! It's the same

excuse used for why blacks don't do as well on the SATs. How long have we been living in America? Come on, people! If we are going to compete in this world (which may be biased), we have to study, read, work, and do whatever we have to do to pass *their* tests. You want to go to "their" schools, pass their tests. You want to work in "their" workforce? Pass their tests.

It's just that simple. And if you don't like it, start your own (which I actually favor).

Those twenty-seven black firefighters from New Haven could have got together and had a study group. They could have found someone who passed the test before and picked his brain.

Now there is a Supreme Court precedent set for reverse-discrimination claims. Now many mainstream corporations have an out for not setting aside positions for blacks. Now they have an excuse *not* to hire us. Thanks, you mediocre, lazy New Haven black firefighters. You're officially part of the problem.

This is why I'm writing this book. We're at a crucial time in our history, and if we don't wake up right now, we stand to lose many of the gains that people died for throughout Jim Crow and the civil rights movement.

All of that marching will have been in vain.

Please Stop!

I'VE BEEN WORKING in the background most of my career—ghostwriting and collaborating on many best-selling and critically acclaimed books, such as *I Make My Own Rules* with LL Cool J, *Ladies First* with Queen Latifah, and *Al on America* with Al Sharpton. I worked at the New York *Daily News* for sixteen years, and even as a columnist I was able to hide behind that picture in the tiny box. My words, while all mine, were muted and oftentimes softened by editors to appeal to the demographics of my paper. I couldn't say exactly what I wanted to say, how I wanted to say it, and that, at times, was frustrating.

By the time I landed on WWRL in 2003 with my own morning talk show, I had learned how to give my opinion in a manner that was palatable. I learned how to have and share my voice while also doing so in a way that allowed others to have theirs. The formula worked. While I never let a guest off the hook—from Hillary Clinton to Ann Coulter, from Michael Steele to the Reverend Jesse Jackson (whom I asked about his out-of-wedlock child)—I was doing so for the listener. I was their champion. I was their advocate. I was their voice.

This book, the kid gloves are off.

For years, I've been blessed to be in the back rooms of big business. I have seen and heard a lot of things. I have done a lot of things that few black people have an opportunity to do—such as start a business with a million-plus dollars from a major Wall Street firm.

What I've learned over the years is that my blackness has power. When I embrace who I am (and this goes for anyone of any ethnicity), I command whatever it is I want to happen. I have been frustrated as I watch black people collectively in so many positions of power simply hand that power over out of fear, out of low self-esteem, and out of a sense of not belonging.

On the one hand, we can get behind a candidate for president and we can hope and we can believe and we can watch him take the highest office in the land.

But on the other hand we watch as our communities crumble, as our households and families are a mess and as our businesses and business base dwindle. How can we, as a people, have so much—perhaps more blacks are in positions of power today than ever before—and yet gain so little?

For me, I can't be successful and think that I'm the exception to the rule and that's okay. Because I was taught at an early age that I am my brother's keeper and that a chain is only as strong as its weakest link. Any success that I have is undermined by the number of blacks enslaved in our prison system, is undermined by the number of blacks not graduating or reading at grade level, is undermined by the number of failed black businesses or the plethora of Korean-owned hair-care places in our communities. My success is undermined unless as part of my success I incorporate reaching back and grabbing folks to go with me.

This crab-in-a-barrel mentality, where we only let a few out at a time or we drag anyone who tries to make it out back in, has got to stop. Now.

I was fortunate to grow up in a household where a notion of community was fostered. My dad had a community corner store in Newark, New Jersey. He kept it open seven days a week, from six in the morning until midnight—rain or shine, holiday or not. His store was in the neighborhood in which he grew up. My grandmother, his mother, lived over the store, as did one of my aunts and five of my cousins.

My father knew just about everyone who came into the store. He had charge accounts: if people didn't have the money, they could get what they needed and pay when they could. He would have little parties during the holidays for the neighborhood at which he gave out gifts and had drinks (alcohol, too), for the customers.

When he was held up on a couple of occasions, he didn't shut down. He understood. He talked to the perpetrators, and on at least one occasion they left without taking anything. He was part of the community, so he felt responsible. He employed young men from the community and taught them about business, how to speak well, how to handle people, how to carry themselves. Each of those young men today is a pillar in his respective community.

Those who lived in the area had a real sense of pride because that store represented their potential. It was clean, it was bright (my father said if lights caused roaches to run, he would have plenty of light inside and outside his store), it was well stocked with fresh food, and it served the people.

I used to go to the store on the weekends, and I got to see firsthand how one person with a heart and a vision could uplift an entire community.

In the summers, I would stay with my grandmother (my mother's mother), who lived in Augusta, Georgia. I used to walk from her dead-end street to the projects where her sister and my aunt Pinkie's nine kids lived. I would spend my days grabbing lunch from the government food lines and playing games that required no money.

While I came from a household where we lacked nothing—we were upper-middle-class—I got to appreciate the other side. I learned to appreciate that money wasn't everything. My aunt Pinkie's house had just as much family and togetherness as any of the Jack-and-Jill homes of my parents' friends.

So this book is much more of a tough-love letter to my people than it is a finger-wagging exploration into what I think is wrong with black folks. Within these pages I want to tell many blacks to wake up, wise up, pay attention to what's really ailing their communities and truly empower themselves.

Every single thing I talk about, I am speaking from experience—from the mistakes I made and from the lessons I learned.

I have earned the right to say the things I will say in this book because I've lived it and I'm the example.

For many years I have been contemplating several versions of this book. It came together for me in the spring of 2007 when radio shock jock Don Imus called the Rutgers women's basketball team "a bunch of nappy-headed hos." Americans (yes, even white folks) lost their minds. For weeks, shows focused on his comments and their fallout. Even Oprah devoted two straight shows and a town hall meeting to talk about race and rap music. Al Sharpton had—what else?—a march before NBC finally capitulated and fired Don Imus.

A march! Are you serious? Al (who is a friend, whom I love dearly as a person) marched over name-calling, but how many marches has he had over the number of black men in jail, the number of black men shooting one another in their neighborhood, the number of black children dropping out of school, or the lack of black businesses in black neighborhoods (oops, let's not bring up Freddy's)?

A LESSON FROM THE BUS BOYCOTTS

When Martin Luther King Jr. and the Southern Christian Leadership Conference and the NAACP were marching, it was for rights and equality. It wasn't over name-calling. I'm sure many *black* people don't even know that the Montgomery bus boycott—which was a huge turning point in the civil rights movement—wasn't only about some back-of-the-bus treatment. They marched and protested and won an integrated system because the white bus companies in Montgomery, Alabama, which found it financially viable to treat blacks like second-class citizens, lost tons of dough as a result of the boycott.

Here's the scoop: Hardworking black folks—many working on their knees cleaning some white person's home or doing some other menial job to put food on the table—had to travel many miles to the white neighborhoods. Blacks were forced to sit in the back of the bus to travel to and from their jobs. But they had to *pay* in the front. So they would get on at the front, pay their nickel or dime, get off, and have to get back on the bus from the back door. On that walk to the back of the bus, the white bus driver would often pull off, leaving the black person out of a ride and out of the money paid for that ride. That's what the boycott was about. Blacks boycotted and marched over being ripped off. They wanted black bus drivers and they wanted not to have to give up a seat if they were already seated in a neutral area between the back and the front just because a white person got on the bus and no more seats were available in the front. It was about respect, but more important, it was about fairness.

There was no "coloreds only" section per se on many buses at the time. It was rarely marked as such. But everyone understood where his or her place was. Front was for the whites and back was for the blacks, and the middle portion of the bus was filled up accordingly: if there was no more room in the front for whites and a black person was the only one sitting in the next row, the black person had to get up and stand in the back.

All the blacks in Montgomery wanted was that if a black person was already seated in the neutral part of the bus, then that row would become a black row. That was it. But the whites refused to negotiate. So a strike was called. The strike went on for more than a year, and the whites still didn't back down. What ended the strike and brought integration to the buses? Economics. One bus company went bankrupt, and the parent company, recognizing where the bulk of their money came from, wanted to capitulate. But by then it was too late.

Bolstered by the *Brown v. Board of Education* decision to integrate schools, and feeling the power of taking their destiny into their own hands, blacks demanded more than just not receiving poor treatment. They demanded equality. The Supreme Court granted them their wish, declaring bus segregation unconstitutional. So in seeking empowerment through using economic might, blacks got even more than they asked for. That's how that works in a capitalist system. Money talks.

Don Imus didn't lose his job because the folks at MSNBC and CBS radio were appalled by his language and didn't want a racist on their network. Don Imus was fired because Procter and Gamble, Staples, GM, Sprint, and several other sponsors pulled their advertising dollars. Imus was first suspended. But when it became cost prohibitive to keep him on the air, the networks "did the right thing."

I believe the best way to effect change is to hit people in the change pocket.

I started writing this book out of frustration. I got

sick and tired of watching my people complain over dumb stuff and not use our ample power to empower our community, and thus a nation. We seemed to get bent out of shape over things we couldn't control, and concerning the things we could control—our neighborhoods, our kids, our schools—we sat on our hands and did nothing (again, there are many individual success stories. I'm talking collectively).

Of course, I'm not happy with what Don Imus said. I am happy, however, that he, Michael ("There's a nigger!") Richards, and the *New York Post* (whose cartoonist Sean Delonas portrayed our president as a chimp) were vilified. But I see it for what it is—hypocrisy on the part of many whites and misplaced energy on the side of many blacks.

I'm not saying we shouldn't say something when folks like Don Imus and Michael Richards or the *New York Post* or anyone else is disrespectful. I just believe that there is a more productive use of energies. I believe if we feel strongly, we should show it by boycotting. Instead of marching and complaining, I believe it's more productive to build wealth, build character, and hone skills. I believe black folks worry so much about what people are saying and calling us, but spend little time on what we are saying and calling each other and even less time on building our communities.

Call me a nigger, a bitch, or a ho, just please get my name right on my checks.

This book will not focus on white people and what they have done. The history of their role in the destruction of a people has been played out a million times. Just pick up a book and read it if you want to be angry about what white people did to just about every group of colored folks, from the Native Americans to the Africans to the Chinese to the East Indians to the American Japanese. I can't control white people. I can only control me.

So this book will focus on what black people need to do to move forward and to improve their lives individually and collectively.

With Obama as president, we are not (as many have suggested) in a postracial society; we are in a hyperracial society where everything, even the shooting of a chimp in Connecticut, becomes fodder for race discussions.

But if we focus on being excellent, and if we focus on cleaning our own homes, if we focus on educating our own children, if we focus on building our own businesses, if we focus on strengthening our own spirituality and being above reproach, it won't matter what anyone does or says as it relates to black people.

Which leads me back to the nuttiness of my people and how misdirected our energies are, and how the title of this book came to be.

I came up with the idea in 1999 while a member of the editorial board of the New York *Daily News*. I was asked to write a piece about a director of the District of Columbia's Office of Public Advocate, who, during a private meeting with his staff, said to his budget aides, "I will have to be niggardly with this fund because it's not going to be a lot of money." One of the aides was black. He was offended by the use of the word *niggardly*. The story made national headlines.

That same year, Amelia Rideau, a student at the University of Wisconsin, was outraged when her four-teenth-century-English professor used *niggardly* in a discussion about poet Geoffrey Chaucer. She called the language offensive and asked that her professor be punished and that the university institute a language code.

I wrote my editorial about how people needed to pick up a dictionary. I talked about how there was real racism, and if people got riled up over a word that *sounded* like another word but wasn't, we're in a heap of trouble.

I thought the issue was dead. But three years later it was back. In 2002, in a North Carolina elementary school, teacher Stephanie Bell decided to use *niggardly* in a spelling class, where the students had to study the word, which would appear on a future test.

I guess she didn't read the 1999 stories about the stir the word raised. Or maybe she did and, like me, found it ridiculous for people to make such a fuss over a word that means "stingy." What was more ridiculous was what happened to Stephanie Bell: she was disciplined, forced by her school administrators to send letters of apology to all of the parents of her students, and had to promise never to use the word again.

The outrage by blacks over the use of the word *niggardly* was hypocritical, misplaced, and ignorant. I couldn't understand why people had to apologize and be threatened with losing their jobs for using a word that means "stingy" or "miserly." Oh, it *sounds* like the word *nigger*. Sure. But the word *nigger* is tossed about so freely in the black community that it has replaced *brother* or *friend* as a greeting or term of endearment. Oh, I get it. *White* people used the word *niggardly*, which sounds like *nigger*. So what? I feel if blacks want to allow other blacks to publicly refer to one another as nigger for all to hear, then they can't be mad if whites do it, too.

But we aren't talking about the word *nigger*. We are talking about *niggardly*—a word I would like to see more blacks embody. Can we be more niggardly with our purchases of shoes, cars, electronics, and bling? Can we?

Black people care about what some dried-up, out-of-touch talk-show host called a group of dignified black women, but when women are called bitches and hos with impunity on neighborhood streets and on multimillion-dollar-selling records, it's cool. Black people want to worry about a teacher or an administrator using *niggardly* in a conversation, but Kanye West can talk about a gold digger not messing with no broke nigger and we throw our hands in the air and wave 'em like we just don't care.

If black people worried more about the sticks and stones being thrown instead of the names they were being called, there would be far fewer problems in the black community!

Herein lies the problem. We can come together to

march and protest over some supposed insult. Meanwhile we sit silently as black kids shoot and beat one another to death in neighborhoods across the country, as hospitals fill up with our babies, abandoned by drug-addicted mothers, while our business base dwindles and while we waste our vast buying power.

So I sat down to start writing, first a column. Then I realized there was so much more to say. I let the subject sit for a while and it evolved. It went from this piece of frustration to this source of pride and hope. Instead of me bitching about black people bitching, I discovered that I could use this book to propel us forward.

INSPIRATION FROM A LITTLE BOOK

In 2005, I was hosting a morning radio show (which I did for three years) in New York City. During my research for my show, I came across an incredible little book that both inspired and saddened me. It was written by a woman named Nannie Helen Burroughs in the 1890s.

She was born to ex-slaves. She pulled herself up by her bootstraps through education and started a school for women, setting a path of self-sufficiency for many in her community. Her book, *Twelve Things the Negro Must Do,* was a prescriptive road map to success for black people. What struck me was that her simple solutions for the well-being of a people more than a hundred years ago were still applicable today.

Tavis Smiley's *Covenant* talked more about the problems. We all know the problems. That's good, because the first step to recovery is to first admit you have a problem. But now it's time to get busy fixing those problems.

I started writing this book about ten years ago out of anger. I was angry that every time I went to a school in my neighborhood to speak, I was told some depressing statistic about low reading scores and poor performers.

I was angry when I would come home to Orange, New Jersey, and end up in confrontations with the neighborhood drug dealer, asking him politely to find another corner. I was angry because I wanted to know if I was the only one who cared enough to say something, and I kept thinking, "Where are the men?"

I was angry driving down Main Street in my town and seeing one Korean-owned hair-care place after another—four, all in the span of three city blocks. I was angry because Koreans don't buy that stuff, black people do. I was angry because Koreans don't even know who Madam C. J. Walker was. She was the first black millionaire in this country and made her fortune off the products that are now owned and controlled by people other than blacks. Why? The answers made me even angrier.

I was angry owning a condo in a building right next door to a rent-controlled complex with more expensive cars in that lot than in ours. I wasn't angry that people wanted nice cars; I was angry that they seemed to prefer having a BMW, Mercedes, or a Lexus over owning a home for themselves and their children. I was angry that people would rather have their children run wild in the streets and in the parking lot rather than take the time to walk them just a few blocks down the street to the newly refurbished park.

I was angry at the bad habits and poor lessons that people were starting their kids off with. I wished I could just shake them and tell them how important it is to give your child a proper foundation—a solid name, strong values, a strong sense of self, and the value of learning and obtaining a solid education.

I got angry when I turned on the television and the vast majority of images depicting black people were of rappers and video hos, Pine-Sol cleaning ladies, and before her transformation, an overweight and dowdy daytime talk-show host.

Then Barack Obama ran for president and I started to get hope. Not that hokey hope that things were going to turn around. But the kind of hope that made me realize that time, and excuses, were running out. If black folks were going to truly matter, beyond simply having "one of us" in the White House, we still had a whole lot of work to do.

So I decided to finish this book.

My anger came from knowing that we can do better—so much better than we're doing.

It is no longer acceptable to point to a few successes and say that it's good enough, because it's not. It's not okay for so many of our children not to get a quality education. It's not okay for too many of our neighborhoods to be overrun with crime and drugs. It's not okay just because it's not happening to you. And it's easy to say, "Well, if people wanted more for their lives, they would work for it."

I used to think that, too. But I also know that sometimes people don't know any better or they haven't had the right impetus to propel them into a better situation.

What I am going to write will not be anything new or unique.

But I know that drops of water on any hard surface will over time wear through that hard surface. I am hoping to be yet another drop of water—just as Nannie Helen Burroughs was a drop of water in her time, as were so many others, from Marcus Garvey to Marva Collins, from Martin to Malcolm (which were more like monsoons), to the preachers and teachers who attempt to inspire and motivate people to live full lives.

I often tell my friends that I want everyone I know to be rich . . . so that nobody has to borrow money from me. Now I'm joking about the borrowing money part (sort of). But the truth is, if people around me are rich in money, in love, in their lives, then they will be happy, and happiness is contagious. I want black people to be happy.

I want everyone to be happy.

The adage is that if America has a cold, black America has pneumonia. The thought is that whatever negatively impacts white or mainstream America can really devastate black America. But what mainstream America fails to see—and it happened most clearly with the drug and HIV epidemics—is that what happens in black America will definitely grip white America. Because, like it or not, we're all in this together.

On 9/11, those flying the planes didn't stop and let the black folks off or the white folks off. They didn't call ahead and tell the blacks to get out of the World Trade Center. No, when those planes struck, they were indiscriminate. They were targeting *Americans*!

Barack Obama became president not because America has grown up, but in spite of her immaturity. He was able to reach the highest office perhaps because he wasn't saddled with the burden of being the son of slaves and the history and stigma that goes with that.

He could, like any immigrant, enjoy all that America had to offer—its opportunity and hope—without the yoke of the slave ties, without the constant reminder of Jim Crow laws that still exist de facto in too many pockets in America. While he was raised by a single mom, his childhood was different from that of the many thousands of black boys raised by single moms throughout America. His mom had him in exotic places such as Hawaii and Indonesia. She exposed him to a variety of cultures and ideas. While their means were limited, his potential was not. He was free . . . free to take hold of whatever his imagination captured for him—including the presidency!

The Emancipation Proclamation freed some of us physically, but the chains that really bind black America are still ever present because they exist in our minds.

It's seen when we "act" different when we're around white people. It's seen in our discomfort at being the "only one" in a room full of whites. It shows up in the classroom when we feel less than or ashamed over what we don't know. It's seen when we place a low value on our work or on our time.

We must confront some of those things and slay the dragon. Free ourselves. It won't start with some law. You cannot legislate morality. Reparations won't do the trick. Don't get me wrong. Black people *are* owed that forty acres and a mule, but that won't change the condition, because we first have to change our own minds.

So this book is about change. It's also about hope. It's about taking a philosophy from a hundred years ago and fulfilling the promise that Nannie Helen Burroughs gave us.

It will start with what *we* must stop doing to ourselves.

I am giving you several things blacks folks must stop doing, followed by Nannie Helen Burroughs's prescriptive *Twelve Things the Negro Must Do*.

I know some of my "suggestions" may rub some people the wrong way. Good. I have learned that change doesn't come in comfort. We make changes when there is pain and discomfort. I want people to be upset, and I want them to talk about it, and I want us to come together and work toward some solutions and make some plans.

I just pray that a hundred years from now neither this book, nor the lessons of Burroughs, will be relevant.

ONE

Stop Complaining and Start Planning

Write down the revelations and make it plain on tablets so that a herald may run with it.

—HABAKKUK 2:2

ON AUGUST 28, 1963, Martin Luther King Jr. stood on the steps of the Lincoln Memorial in Washington, D.C., and delivered a speech that will go down in history as one of the most powerful, poignant, and inspired speeches of our time. It is known as the "I Have a Dream" speech and it begins:

Five score years ago, a great American, in whose symbolic shadow we stand, signed the Emancipation Proclamation. This momentous decree came as a great beacon light of hope to millions of Negro slaves who had been seared in the flames of withering injustice. It came as a joyous daybreak to end the long night of captivity.

But one hundred years later, we must face the tragic fact that the Negro is still not free. One hundred years later, the life of the Negro is still sadly crippled by the manacles of segregation and the chains of discrimination. One hundred years later, the Negro lives on a lonely island of poverty in the midst of a vast ocean of material prosperity. One hundred years later, the Negro is still languishing in the corners of American society and finds himself an exile in his own land. So we have come here today to dramatize an appalling condition.

As you will see with Nannie Helen Burroughs's powerfully instructive message, not much has changed for black folks in America in a hundred years. Sure, much of the struggle of the 1960s led to changes in the laws that allowed blacks to drink from whatever water fountain they chose or to ride in the front of the buses. These laws even gave blacks the right to vote. But what changed economically for blacks?

- Black family income is at an all-time high, but is still only 58 percent of that of the average family in America.

- According to the Federal Reserve, the wealth gap between whites and African-Americans is widening. According to the Fed, for every dollar of wealth held by a typical white family in 2007, a black family had only ten cents— that's two cents less than the family had in 2004.
- And with layoffs in 2009 affecting blacks disproportionately, that gap is expected to increase even more.
- Black-owned businesses have increased in number and have penetrated a wide range of industries over the past thirty years. But the sales of the one hundred largest black-owned businesses combined are less than the sales of any one of the companies on the Fortune 500 list of major industrial corporations. Outside of *Black Enterprise*, TV One (which is limping), and *Ebony* and *Jet* (which are on life support as I'm writing this), blacks own no major media outlets.
- Equal pay? While blacks have made progress over the last thirty years, African-Americans still earn about seventy-four cents for every dollar a white

person earns. And in 2004, black family income was
58 percent of that of white families—a drop from
63 percent in 1974.

In that "I Have a Dream" speech, King also said:

In a sense we have come to our nation's capital to cash
a check. When the architects of our republic wrote
the magnificent words of the Constitution and the
Declaration of Independence, they were signing a
promissory note to which every American was to fall
heir.

That's not true. The framers of the Constitution and
the Declaration of Independence at no time considered blacks—who were then slaves—to be a part of
the America they were building. Blacks were chattel,
property, three-fifths of a man. There was certainly no
consideration of their rights or needs, nor were they
considered "heirs" to all the wealth that was to become
America's.

Here's where King's dream has continued to be just
that. Having a dream, instead of having a plan, has rele-
gated us to living in a world of fantasy instead of reality.

Now, I'm not criticizing King or his speech because he was able to get Americans—both black and white—to really start to see black people as equal and deserving participants in this democracy, and that was important. His agenda was not about economic empowerment or even black pride, as was the push by Marcus Garvey and later Malcolm X. We need to dream. Dreams are the building blocks to the manifestation of real accomplishments.

But after we finish dreaming, we need to wake up and do something!

If King had lived, perhaps his work would have evolved. Instead of hoping for white acceptance and unity, he would have rallied blacks to create their own industries and develop their own base of wealth. He would have talked about economic empowerment—not what the government "owes" blacks but what we blacks owe ourselves.

Instead of talking about integrating schools, King might have seen that perhaps talking about making all-black schools better—making them schools that could rival those of whites—would have been more productive. Instead of calling for integrated neighborhoods, he might have talked about making black neighborhoods places where even white people would fight to get in.

Instead of blacks complaining about having to drink from the broken-down COLOREDS ONLY fountains, King could have urged blacks to create their own elaborate fountains in their own neighborhoods.

Yes, Rosa Parks was tired and didn't want to give up her seat or stand in the back of the bus. But why didn't blacks create their own bus system? Start it off with some vans. If everyone had chipped in to buy that first bus, the people would have been able to buy a fleet of buses from the monies made.

Martin Luther King Jr. spoke of a dream, and it was a nice speech, a great speech, an inspiring speech. But I believe his speech and his dream was supposed to manifest into something greater, and we've let King down.

We had to have the dream. But what would have pushed the black cause further would have been a plan—an economic plan to go along with the dream.

I am a dreamer by nature. I sit around from time to time imagining my next conquest, my next journey, and I play it out in my mind. I fantasize about the wealth I will have and the schools I will build and the children I will take care of.

But I live by a plan. I learned that words are powerful. In the beginning of the Bible it says that God *said* let there be light and there was. He didn't think about light and it happened. He *said* something and it happened. Words then must be the key to accomplishment, followed by action.

I learned that by writing down the things that I dreamed about and envisioned, they often came to fruition. I guess you can equate it to going on a trip and having an idea of where you are going but not having a map. If you're on a trip without a map and you get lost, you can certainly pull over and ask someone for directions, but you run the risk of someone sending you even farther out of your way with bad advice. The best thing you can do is to make sure you have a map—a clear map—that shows you exactly where you are and where you need to be before you even set out on your journey.

WRITING DOWN THE DREAM

In 1996, I'd got off track, even with some of the positive examples I had from my youth. I was in a bad place financially, spiritually, and physically. My weight had got out of control. I was pushing 240 pounds, eating things I don't even look at today. My gallbladder eventually had to be removed. I was making bad choices in my personal and financial life.

I turned to a friend who had been studying the Bible and started talking about the things that were going on in my life. My friend asked me a simple question: "What do you want to happen in your life?"

I said, "I want everything to be on the right track. I want peace."

"Well, first *you* have to be on the right track," my friend told me. "You have to take a good hard look at yourself and see where you are. Then you have to look inside yourself and determine where you want to be, and then you have to write it down and look at it every day. And I guarantee you, you will get there."

So I soul-searched and came up with seven goals:

1. Get closer to God/peace, wisdom through Him
2. Health/booming shape
3. Find love (learn to give and receive)/passion
4. Write a book
5. Buy a house (Arlington Avenue)

6. Get an SUV(Land Rover Defender 90 or Discovery)/Saab (I want back what I had lost)
7. Have fun/enjoy life/make new friends

These goals I typed on my computer January 1, 1996, printed them out, and placed them in my daily planner, which I started using for all of my personal and business efforts since 1991. I taped a copy of my goals on the inside cover so that every day, when I opened my planner to write a number or record a meeting or some other important date, I would be forced to look at it.

By the end of the year, I was definitely getting closer to God. I started studying the Bible. I had read it before but it had just seemed like a bunch of stories in the past. This time as I was reading, I didn't start at the beginning and read it as I would a book. I started in the back with the words in red (in my NIV edition) and studied the things Jesus said and got a deeper understanding of the nature of God and what He expected of me. I learned how to hear from God through reading His word.

Physically, I hadn't lost much weight and I hadn't found love, but I did write a book. I didn't get that dream house on Arlington Avenue in East Orange, New

Jersey, but I did get a new car, a Toyota 4Runner, and I made a few new friends. I was able to cross off four things on my list of seven and I was encouraged.

The following year, I got bold. My goals:

1. Have a really deep relationship with God
2. Become disciplined
3. Get out of debt
4. Write another book or two
5. Buy a house or a condo
6. Make more than $100,000 annually
7. Start a business
8. Write a column at a major newspaper

And at the bottom of my list of goals, I mapped out all of my creditors, the people I owed money to, with the account numbers and the amount owed—everyone from American Express at $13,891 to the IRS at $1,458 to the $3,000 that I owed in parking tickets.

As I started to pay these off, I would put a line through the bills—crossing off my debt and at the same time freeing my spirit.

I finally got paid for my work on *I Make My Own Rules* with LL Cool J, and it did so well that I even got two bonus checks. With that money, I crossed off No. 3 on my list of goals and all of the line items that I had on the bottom of the page that were left. I also had enough for a down payment on a condominium. I crossed off No. 5 and with my salary, I was able to cross off No. 6, too. Goal No. 4 took a little work, and I didn't see that come to fruition until the following year. No. 1 and No. 2, I decided, would be lifelong processes that I would never cross off.

Sometimes you will find that your goals from one year don't happen until years later. Going back into my daily planners from 1996 until today, I see that every single one of the things that I wrote down has happened—from starting a business (which I did in 1999 with a million dollars from a group of Wall Street investors and again in 2007 with a publishing house), to having a column (which was officially awarded to me by the New York *Daily News* in 2001), to having a banging body (it took me until 2007 to get to a decent weight; I'm still working on the banging part). It is a process, and that process began with having a daily plan to do something, even if just one thing, such as not to eat that bagel for breakfast, that would help me accomplish one of my larger goals.

The process began with a plan, then making that plan plain in writing for me to look at every day.

While having a dream is a wonderful thing—a vision is important—having a plan is the only certain way to realize that dream.

TAKING ON THE PUBLISHERS

In 2006, I decided to start my third business.

After writing books as a collaborator for a number of years, I had circulated a couple of proposals to several large publishing houses for books that I believed in. The projects kept getting rejected. It was funny because if I wrote a proposal for a celebrity book or some tell-all, I would easily get a six-figure deal, but if I wanted to write a book that I believed would inspire young black kids across the country, I was told by at least one publisher, "Black kids don't read!"

I knew my response was valid: "Black kids don't read because publishers don't produce the kinds of books that interest them."

They still didn't budge. Instead of complaining about how publishers were shortsighted and cry about how they didn't produce the kinds of books for "our" kids that could reach them, I decided to start my own house.

I had a vision that my house would rival Simon & Schuster, Random House, and Penguin.

I know. Who in the world did I think I was? I was just a black woman whose only publishing experience had been in collaborating on a few bestselling books as a writer. I had zero publishing experience. But I had a vision, just like Richard Simon and Max Schuster, two guys who started publishing crossword puzzles and expanded from there, and just like Bennett Cerf, Christopher Coombes, and Donald Klopfer, who started Random House in 1927. As Cerf would say, "We just said we were going to publish a few books on the side at random."

I was going to start a publishing house that would produce books that motivated and inspired and entertained people.

Again, I wrote on paper my mission:

- Publish books that I don't see in the market.
- Find and create new, hot authors who had stories to tell that would inspire, motivate, and entertain.
- Be true to who I am.

I had no idea what I was getting myself into. I didn't have any family or friends who had been in this industry whom I could rely on to guide me. I knew I would make plenty of mistakes, but I also knew that with a vision and a plan I was more than halfway there. The next thing I did was to approach some of those huge publishing houses. I called St. Martin's Press, Random House/Doubleday, and Simon & Schuster. I received a call back from Carolyn Reidy, the president of Simon & Schuster. She was interested in hearing what I had to say. She gave me a couple of options of imprints that I could work with. I chose Pocket Books. The publisher of Pocket, Louise Burke, was a straight shooter with so much experience that I wanted to soak up everything she had to offer.

I knew what I didn't know, and if I planned on having a house big enough to one day compete with the big guys, I needed to be armed with knowledge that I could only get from the source.

I hear people in my neighborhood complain about the businesses they see. Just about every other corner has a Korean hair-care place, a Korean nail establishment, a Chinese take-out joint, or a convenience store run by a person from the Middle East. I have heard complaints about how people come into our neighbor-hood and start businesses and blah, blah, blah.

While I can easily jump on that interloper band-wagon, instead I ask this question: "What are *you* doing about it?"

Are you dreaming and planning and doing? Or are you just complaining?

TWO

Stop Tearing Down Our Heroes

*How important it is for us to recognize and celebrate
our heroes and she-roes!*

—MAYA ANGELOU

IN 2007, OPRAH Winfrey announced the opening of
her leadership academy in South Africa. I was invited
to speak on a panel on CNN about whether Oprah was
right to do this, or if she should be spending her money
in America on American children. Many columnists—
mostly black—around the country were criticizing the
media mogul for doing something that I hadn't seen
too many people doing—lending a hand to change
the lives of young black people. I contemplated not
going on CNN. I didn't want to validate the notion that
something might actually be wrong with what Oprah
was doing. But I decided to go on and throw in my two
cents.

My points: (1) It's Oprah's money. If she wanted to build a monument to herself in the middle of South Africa on land she purchased and it cost her $50 million, that was her business. (2) Out of all the people criticizing, how many of them had actually lifted a finger to educate, inspire, and/or motivate a child in need? Why target someone for criticism who, instead of talking about a problem, is actually rolling up her silky sleeves and doing something about it?

Even with the controversy surrounding the school, Oprah's intentions were to do something great to help young lives.

Then I talked about the millions Oprah had given for scholarships to children in *America*—such as the fund she has at Morehouse to educate young black men.

I often wonder if Martin Luther King Jr., Malcolm X, and Adam Clayton Powell Jr. were alive today, would they have been able to accomplish the things they accomplished? (And scandal certainly gripped Powell even back then.) I wondered if there was a skeleton in Thurgood Marshall's closet, would he have even made it to the Supreme Court? The great writers of yesterday— the James Baldwins and the Lorraine Hansberrys and the Langston Hugheses—would we be honoring them in today's climate?

Would every detail of their every human actions and errors be ripped apart, examined, and splayed for all to read in the media? Would they be followed by paparazzi? Would they be on the covers of our tabloids every week?

Probably.

If that had happened, would they still be our heroes? Would we celebrate their birthdays, name streets for them, read about them in our history books?

This isn't just about black folks. We, as a nation, are hero killers. If George Washington and Thomas Jefferson were alive today, we would be so consumed with their personal lives and their addictions and frailties that I doubt they would ever be allowed to be great.

Bill Clinton's presidency has an asterisk that John F. Kennedy's would easily have got had his presidency been during the same time.

We seem so caught up in gossip and scandal that we forget that people *are* human.

We are all human beings and we all fall short of the grace of God. That said, in our humanity, in our flaws, is where true greatness lies. For a person to overcome his inequities to do great things makes him even greater.

But we have a mentality where we love to see people rise up from nowhere, but if they get too big, we delight more in their fall, and in tearing them down.

It's impossible to have heroes in that environment. And without heroes, we have no foundation for a great society. Without heroes, we don't have a history.

Oprah Winfrey should be one of the greatest inspirations of our times, yet so much that is negative is written about her. A recent article even alleged some cocaine use in her past. Who cares? Does that change the impact she has had on changing the face of media, and her inspiration and motivation of so many people to reach their potential?

They will talk about the scandal surrounding her South African school. They will talk about how her father wrote a tell-all book about her. I believe Oprah will still be one of our great Americans when it's all said and done, but not without tarnish. ("Yeah, what's really up with her and Gayle?" will be the tagline.)

Is this all about keeping it real or telling the truth, or do we do this dance in tearing people down to make ourselves feel better about the things we have not accomplished or the things we think we cannot accomplish?

BACKLASH AGAINST
BONDS AND 'BAMA

Barry Bonds. Whether he did steroids or not, the reality is that he was an incredible baseball player—perhaps the best to ever play. If steroids gave people such an edge, how come no one else is even close to breaking Hank Aaron's home-run record? Mark McGwire, Sammy Sosa, Jason Giambi, Alex Rodriguez, Manny Ramirez—they are all accused, and none of them have come close to catching Bonds.

It is called the Steroid Era because of the drug's rampant use. So where are the others threatening perhaps the most prestigious and definitely most difficult record to break?

Because steroids don't give you talent. They allow you to lift weights longer, which makes you stronger and perhaps faster, but they don't give you the skill or the hand-eye coordination that it takes to hit home runs or to pitch. That's why steroids only really matter in track and field and swimming, and maybe football, where speed and strength are the main ingredients for success. (And of course, professional wrestling . . . but that's not real, is it?)

Who cares if a golfer is on steroids? It certainly wouldn't help a basketball player much. And if it were that big a deal in baseball, you would definitely have had more than Sammy Sosa, Mark McGwire, and Barry Bonds breaking home-run records. Jason Giambi, a known steroids user, wasn't even the third-best player on the Yankees. He will never break any records. If we're keeping it real, Babe Ruth, Ty Cobb, and Mickey Mantle should have asterisks next to their records and accolades, too, because they amassed their records against inferior talent. The best players were in the Negro League, which these men never played against. How can a person be the greatest if he never played against the best?

But America gets to keep their heroes intact. I will never say that the drunk Babe Ruth, the drunk Mickey Mantle, and the racist Ty Cobb don't deserve to be American baseball heroes, because they do. And so does Barry Bonds.

Barack Obama ran for president—I mean he *really* ran for president. It wasn't a publicity stunt to simply push an agenda. He wanted to lead this nation. And what do black people do? They start questioning whether he's black enough.

A black man has a real shot at the White House, and some of his own people start throwing darts. That was the dumbest thing I'd ever seen. If he wasn't black enough, Obama was at least blacker than his opponents—Hillary Clinton, Chris Dodd, John Edwards, and Joseph Biden, as if any of those candidates would do more for black people than Obama.

Instead of praising and exalting this man, who has an incredible mind and an incredible background, who also happened to be black (he fit the rule of being more than one thirty-second black; he probably has more "black blood" than many of you reading this book), the discussion centered around his being raised by a white woman in Hawaii and by white grandparents and whether he could relate to the African-American plight.

Question: if it's late at night and Barack Obama is standing in midtown Manhattan heading to Harlem, will he easily be able to hail a cab? No? Then he's black!

I'm not saying that black people should have supported Barack Obama simply because he's black (and blacks did finally jump on the bandwagon after white America said it was okay in Iowa). But holding him to a "black" standard that no other candidate had to live up to was simply wrong. And dumb! Could we have allowed the man to show who he was and what he was made of before we tore him down?

Thank goodness the black backlash early in Obama's run didn't stop him from becoming the forty-fourth president of the United States of America. But it could have.

That the scrutiny was even there to begin with (and for those with a short memory, do a little research into the early days of the Obama campaign and see how black folks were talking about him then) is disheartening.

I believe some black folks acted like that because they have been programmed to hate themselves. It's not something conscious—it's just two to three hundred years' worth of being devalued to the point where some of us cannot believe that anything black is worthy of success. We don't believe that we ourselves are worthy.

Some buy into the same divide-and-conquer mentality that whites used on us for so many years. It's why Africans don't like African-Americans, Guyanese don't like Trinidadians, Puerto Ricans can't stand Dominicans, and Dominicans hate Haitians. My struggle is greater than yours!

It's also unfair and inconsistent to make some blacks take the black test while others get a free ride.

If certain blacks have to pass some sort of blackness test, then a whole bunch of other so-called black leaders need to be examined equally. Let's talk about Jesse Jackson, for example.

Jesse Jackson is supposed to be a reverend and a spiritual leader, in addition to being a civil rights activist. He says a few rhymes and holds a few marches and all's cool. No one says, "Hey, wait a minute!" when he reportedly fathered a (and by some reports more than one) child out of wedlock. He still gets invited to preach at churches on Sunday and has yet to have to really answer to that. So he gets to be a hero?

Let's be consistent. Either everyone gets the microscope treatment or no one does. As a people, black folks don't have the luxury of kicking people off the island because they're not black enough. (One exception: Clarence Thomas.) And we don't have the luxury not to have heroes. We need them. We need the Oprahs and the Obamas so that the next generation can have someone to look up to and strive to be.

Martin, Malcolm, and Adam inspired so many of the leaders of today to pick up their mats and walk and serve the community. Without Thurgood Marshall there would not have been a Johnnie Cochran. I am a writer today because of Maya Angelou and her caged-bird song.

THE QUIET HEROES

Most of our heroes of today may never be remembered in our history books, however, because they do their work away from the spotlight, not seeking attention and accolades. We need to build those people up, give our children something to shoot for. A rapper can't be a hero just because he wrote a great rhyme, though a few definitely transcend being entertainers and deserve a mention. A supermodel shouldn't be idolized just because she takes a nice picture and can strut her stuff on the runway. Nor should singers or any other performers be heroes just because they're famous and talented.

We have to begin to redirect attention away from those empty vessels and focus on the real heroes—those right in front of our faces that we attempt to destroy by delighting in their failures whenever they happen.

In addition to our stopping to tear down our heroes, we need to raise up some that we rarely hear about. We need to make sure our children know who their heroes are in their community. I'm talking about such people as the great parents, teachers, and community activists. I'm also talking about folks who are doing tremendous work but have to kill somebody to get some press. We have to make sure we spread the word in our communities about the likes of:

Dr. Ben Carson, the best pediatric neurosurgeon in the country. He was classified as a special ed student while growing up in the projects of Detroit with an illiterate mother. But he persevered and is one of the greatest doctors of our time. Will we name a street for him one day? I hope so.

Neil deGrasse Tyson, head of the Hayden Planetarium. In 2006, he declassified Pluto as a planet. A black man, through his research decided that Pluto would no longer be considered a planet, and it will be wiped out of the history books. When will we celebrate his day?

Marva Collins, who left the Chicago school system because she didn't believe it cared about the children and founded her own school. She took the worst kids from the worst neighborhoods and taught them philosophy and to believe in themselves. One of the students in her Westside Preparatory School was labeled borderline retarded by the Chicago school system, but went on to graduate from college summa cum laude. Her students have degrees from Harvard, Yale, Stanford, and Oxford. Many of her students have gone on to become physicians, lawyers, engineers, and educators. Why hasn't she been considered for secretary of education for this failing system of ours in America—which lags behind those of eighteen other industrialized nations?

I could go on for pages listing people who have done tremendous things in our community, yet we focus on rapper T.I. getting arrested for having a machine gun or whether Janet Jackson is pregnant.

"We don't control the media."

I have heard this lament on quite a few occasions.

But that's not necessarily true. It goes back to what I said in the previous chapter about how money talks. With our dollars and our eyeballs we can dictate what we see in the media. We can utilize write-in campaigns and rally the troops to force the powers in the media to make some changes. We can stop purchasing newspapers or visiting websites that routinely denigrate our much needed heroes for the sake of a quick buck. Remember, backlash and action got Imus fired from MSNBC.

Even if we don't control the media, we do control what we say about one another and what we choose to allow people to say about us. In this age of constant twittering, facebooking, and myspacing, let's think about what we're saying about each other, and, instead, to paraphrase an entertainer who wrote a heroic song two decades ago, let's look at the woman or the man in the mirror.

I contributed to a book in 2005 that I wish I hadn't. In 2007, this person released her second book and it shot to No. 6 on the *New York Times* bestseller's list. I wasn't surprised by its success, but I was saddened by it. When I worked on the first book with her, my goal was to present a story of a woman who chose a life that was so tragic that any young girl out there wanting to be seen in music videos would think twice before following in those stilettos. I hoped this cautionary tale would help the author look inside herself and want more for her life.

Unfortunately, just the opposite happened. If I can do anything toward undoing that, it is my hope that this chapter will get us to start thinking more about the positive things that people are doing and to stop tearing down our heroes.

We all bear a responsibility in this. The things we do matter. What we say matters.

THREE

Stop Blaming Bill Cosby
(And Anyone Else Telling the Truth!)

I don't know the key to success, but the key to failure is trying to please everybody.

—BILL COSBY

A word to the wise ain't necessary—it's the stupid ones that need the advice.

—BILL COSBY

IN 2005, MICHAEL Eric Dyson wrote a book called *Is Bill Cosby Right?: Or Has Black Middle Class America Lost Its Mind?* The book did fairly well and garnered some attention for the author, who made the rounds lambasting Bill Cosby for comments he had made in public criticizing blacks for everything from the names they give their children to too many father's not accepting responsibility in raising their kids.

Whether Bill Cosby was on the wrong side of the race issue in the 1960s when he integrated television (and in many circles is credited with opening a whole bunch of doors), whether, as Dyson pointed out, Cosby was black enough back then, or whether his portrayal of black America with *The Cosby Show* was realistic, it cannot be argued that Bill Cosby made a difference. His presence mattered.

The things he has said about what blacks need to do and what blacks need to stop doing are worthy of discussion. Who cares what white America thinks? Black America has some issues.

I did a book with Al Sharpton during his run for president in 1999. In that book in discussing rap music, the Reverend Al made a profound statement in taking rappers to task. He said that rappers talk about keeping it real and they talk about rap being a mirror of what's going on in society. "Well, when I look in the mirror, I don't just leave the house with my hair messed up and stuff on my face," he said. "When I look in the mirror, it's with an eye on fixing what I see. I try to correct the image that I see in the mirror."

What he was saying is that it's a cop-out to make excuses for negative and damaging images that are projecting to the world (because in the case of rap and hip-hop, people listen to it in Japan, Germany, and Australia as much if not more than we do in the United States) and simply say, "Well, I'm just mirroring what I see."

When you have a platform and a medium that can be shared with millions, you also have a responsibility to make a positive change and correct some of the things you see that you do not like. That's true power.

So Bill Cosby said some things. Were they true? Is it irresponsible to saddle a child with the name Shaniqua and expect that child to be successful? Yes, Barack Obama may change all of that. Maybe. But maybe not. More important, Cosby's real message was that we shouldn't give children names that have no meaning. Barack means something. It means "blessed" or "blessed by God." What does Shaniqua or Shanaynay mean? What Cosby was saying is that you should put some thought into what you name your child. It should have some purpose. Naming a kid Alizé or Moët because that's your favorite drink is akin to child abuse. Why should a child have to defend the crazy decision by his or her parent(s) for the rest of his or her life?

In 2009, a Jersey couple had their three children

removed from their home. They had named their children Adolf Hitler, JoyceLynn Aryan Nation, and Honszlynn Hinler Jeannie. The state deemed these parents unfit. And I agree. But I also believe that anyone naming their child after their favorite liquor or automobile should be brought up on child abuse charges, too.

And if someone has the boldness to call people on their stupidity, that person should not be held up to ridicule and examination.

My question to Michael Eric Dyson and anyone else who wants to throw darts at Bill Cosby is, what have you done for the community? Whom have you personally helped to succeed?

I do not know Bill Cosby. I have never met him in person. But I have seen him several times—in my community! I swim at a pool in Newark, New Jersey. It's free and open to the public, and on my way to JFK Pool one day, the street I needed to turn down was blocked with police cars. I thought, "Oh, no, what happened now." After all, it is Newark. I pulled up to one of the officers and asked what was going on. He told me that Bill Cosby was there to speak to the kids. This was a middle school in the middle of Newark. There were no media alerts, no press releases, no news stories. I didn't

see a single news truck. There was no fanfare, except
for the police presence. Bill Cosby just showed up to
talk to the kids.

A new jazz/nightclub opened in West Orange, New
Jersey, a black-owned establishment. For one week Bill
Cosby appeared there, free of charge, to help this man
put his club, Cecil's, on the map. There are a bunch of
stories like that where Bill Cosby just shows up.

The Cosby Show helped change the image of black
folks following an era of *Good Times* and blaxploitation
films and made it palatable for blacks to be perceived as
educated, progressive, wealthy, family-oriented people.
If the show did just that, it would have been enough.
Bill Cosby could have rested on his laurels. (Let's not
mention how many black kids aspired to attend college
after *A Different World* aired.)

Instead, he decided to not sit at home, but to get out
in the community and talk about the things he felt were
important. Is Bill Cosby right all of the time? No. None
of us is. But he has earned the right to say the things
he has said without people such as Dyson trying to take
him down. Bill Cosby isn't perfect, but we can't expect
to wait on perfect people to deliver a message. Jesus
came already.

Don't you hate it when you're arguing with people and you're right, but instead of their dealing with the points of that argument, they bring up something you might have done in the past and try to completely reverse the discussion? That's what Dyson did in his book.

We need to deal with the black family and why so many men aren't taking care of their children. Even Barack Obama spoke to this issue. We need to deal with our lack of education and the almost embarrassment experienced by those who are highly educated who fear not being accepted by their own culture. What's up with that? I can't imagine that a people who risked life and limb to learn to read during a time when they could be killed for knowledge are raising a generation of children who refuse to read for fear of looking like a nerd. Are we serious? And Bill Cosby can't talk about that?

We need to talk about that, and who cares if white people or any other people are listening. Again, we do not have the luxury to not look in the mirror and fix what we see that's wrong. In the Obama era, black folks need to strive for excellence now more so than ever before. The world is watching. Let's show our best.

Instead of being defensive when someone tells us

our breath is stinking, how about brushing the teeth, flossing, or popping in a mint or checking your diet. Don't kill the messenger.

We need to stop doing that. We need to stop blaming Bill Cosby (and anyone else telling the truth)!

FOUR

Stop Dividing

*Divide and conquer—that's what they try to do to
any group trying to make social change. I call it
D&C. Black people are supposed to turn against
Puerto Ricans. Women are supposed to turn
against their mothers and mothers-in-law. We're all
supposed to compete with each other for the favors
of the ruling class.*

—FLORYNCE R. KENNEDY, lawyer, activist

*So the same cultural and political issues that divided
us in 1968 are still dividing us.*

—RUSSELL BANKS, writer

ONE OF MY students at Hunter College where I teach
media asked me, "Are you West Indian?"

"Why?" I was curious.

"Because you sure do work a lot of jobs!"

At the time I was teaching a couple of classes at Hunter College, hosting a morning radio show, and writing books.

I wanted to be flattered, but I needed to understand the root of the question. This student was West Indian, and I guess it would have been a source of pride for her to "claim" me as one of her own, or to validate her notion that West Indians were somehow more hardworking than American blacks.

The more I thought about the question and the motivation behind it, the more disturbed I became. So I decided to toss a few questions back at her.

"Are you West Indian?"

"Yes!" she proudly claimed. "I'm Trinidadian!"

"Are you sure?"

She looked at me, puzzled. "Yes, I'm sure."

"So what's a West Indian?"

Before I allowed her to answer, I had to give her a quick lesson in history and geography. I had to explain to her something she must have known but, like many of us, just didn't ever process. I explained how the boats sailed from Africa and how they dropped off some of their cargo (black folks) in what we call Central and South America, came up the Atlantic and dropped off more in what we call the Caribbean or what was once called the West Indies (which Columbus supposedly found), and then the boats either moved back and forth from Africa to the West Indies or came directly, thanks to slave-ship magnates such as the Brown brothers, who founded Brown University, to America with their cargos—Africans.

"So, you're not West Indian, you're an African dropped off in the West Indies," I told her. "We're the same people."

I saw in her this desire to protest and I understood. People have this sick sense. They want to feel better or superior to the next person. It's the root cause of racism. Black folks understand it when it comes to white people, but the racism that exists among blacks is what is really killing us.

It goes back to slavery and the division between house slaves and field slaves. The slave owners knew what they were doing when they gave preferential treatment to the house slaves (many of whom were the result of relations that the slave owners had with field slaves). It's called divide and conquer, an age-old and effective tactic. If you can get a people to fight among themselves, then they are easier to defeat. So for two hundred-plus years the slave owners fostered this mind-set that house slaves, who were lighter-skinned, of course, were "better" than the field slaves.

Postslavery in America, a paper-bag test was given for membership into certain black fraternities, sororities, and other organizations. If you were lighter than a brown paper bag, you got in. If you were darker, you didn't.

Today we do it with this "cultural" division where Africans and West Indians come to America and feel superior or have this notion that they are more hardworking or smarter, etc., than American blacks.

But I will ask them all a few questions: Why did you leave where you came from? If "your" people were all that wonderful and smart and hardworking, what brought you to America? Why didn't your great people have a great society for you to make a living in and take care of yourself and your family?

There is no "your" people and "my" people. That's the answer. There is no West Indian. And there is no Hispanic or Latino. Close your mouths.

If you're not a Spaniard from Spain, meaning European, you, too, are an African dropped off in a Spanish-speaking place. Yes, some of you are Indian or indigenous people. But most of you are Africans. People don't know that a majority of Mexicans are of African descent (and the existence of pyramids there is not simply a coincidence). Now, the Spaniards used miscegenation as a form of conquering. Theirs was a powerful form of divide and conquer. So many Puerto Ricans and Central and South Americans do have Spanish blood (whatever that means). But according to the definition of black in America—which is, if you are one thirty-second black, you are black—most of you so-called Latinos are black!

I've gotten into quite a few arguments about this, which also puzzles me. So-called Latinos will argue to beat the band if you try to call them black. I want to know why. What's wrong with being black? Really!

One more question for you so-called Hispanics. If you went to Spain tomorrow and ran up on a Spaniard, would he consider you Spanish? Hell no! So what are you? Puerto Rican? Dominican? Those aren't races, they are regions. Just because you speak Spanish doesn't make you Spanish! Pelé, the greatest soccer player ever, spoke Spanish. Was he black or Spanish?

I have a friend, Leland Hardy, who is as fluent in Mandarin Chinese as any Chinese person. But that doesn't make him Chinese. He's black! And so are most Puerto Ricans and so are most Dominicans (especially Dominicans).

With Dominicans it would seem a no-brainer, right? Where is the Dominican Republic on the map? Oh. It shares the exact same island with Haiti! Yet those on the Dominican side of the island of Hispaniola are detached from their Haitian roots. They feel superior to their poor, downtrodden brothers on the other side. Please, people, pick up a history book and read, just a little.

Here's the deal: The Haitians were the first group of Africans, *the first,* to gain their independence from their captors! What does that mean? It means these are some pretty special people. It is the only nation formed by a successful slave revolt. Imagine the slaves on this island taking on the mighty Napoléon and his French forces and winning! And you wonder why Haiti catches so many blows today? The powers that be in the world couldn't reward this slave colony—despite its organization, its brilliance, its resources. They had to make it pay for its arrogance and audacity to not just crave freedom but do something about it. Many attempts were made across the seas and in the New World to fight for freedom (Nat Turner led perhaps the most notable revolt in America), but they all ended in defeat—except for Haiti.

And these other nations, including the one sharing Haiti's space, have the gall to look down their noses on these people? All they are doing is perpetuating that same negative image that so many hoped to project, and they have allowed themselves to be further conquered.

How powerful would the island of Hispaniola be if the folks on the Dominican Republic side teamed up with the folks on the Haiti side? Nature tells me there's strength in numbers. But instead, generations of Dominicans have been raised to not mix with darker-skinned people and to look down on the folks of Haiti.

All of you brown and light brown people who speak Spanish are black. Think about that. You can mix with white folks all you want and you will never erase the truth. So you might as well embrace it because that's where your true strength and power lies.

Realize that you are a pawn. You are being used by the power base in America to form a separate group so that the black bloc won't be so powerful. You are contributing to your own demise.

Imagine if the so-called Latinos woke up and recognized that they are what they actually are—black! What would happen to the numbers game that they play in politics?

Divide and conquer!

It's all about power. For years white America has got away with playing with the numbers to maintain their majority. Let's look at the founding fathers—good old red-blooded white Anglo-Saxon Protestants. Then the Irish came. Well, they didn't quite measure up to the standards of being white. In the South, many of them were indentured servants who lived worse than a slave. In the North, they were considered niggers. But then the Italians came, and it was prudent for the Irish to graduate to whiteness. The Italians were then considered the next niggers.

In between all of them were the Jews. I often have similar conversations with Jews to the ones I have with Hispanics. Many Jews in this country are under the impression that they are white, too. And they are, only when it's convenient. But World War II should have taught them a valuable lesson about how white people perceive racial purity. That whole eugenics idea that Hitler attempted to carry out came from a few Harvard professors and American doctors. It was an *American* idea first.

How many boatloads of Jews escaping Germany were sent back to face their death? Did America jump into that war against Hitler because he was exterminating Jews? No! So why do Jews think that they are really accepted as white people in America today? Money, power, and social position didn't save them in Hitler's Germany, and they had it all. If it hits the fan here, watch what happens.

I say all of this to point out that most of us live in a fantasy world when it comes to race. We believe that ours is the exception. If you're from the Caribbean, you believe that white people perceive you as more acceptable than American blacks. If you're from Africa, you may feel the same. Those of you who consider yourselves Hispanic and urge your offspring to stay away from "niggers" because you want to whiten your future generations, please stop. Please embrace your heritage.

Because before there was a white person, this world was ruled by people with black and brown skins.

Before there was a Columbus, there was Abubakari II, who sailed the ocean blue, all the way to Mexico (and there were those Africans before him, which is why there are pyramids there. And maize sculptures in

Egyptian tombs). But Abubakari II didn't feel the need to "conquer" a people who already existed. Neither he nor those before him felt the need to put a flag there and say they discovered something that was already there. Before white people were ruling the world, they were in caves, while black folks were kings and queens with intricate political structures and aqueducts and successful governments.

Everyone gets his or her turn on top, is my point.

My ultimate point is that we divide ourselves or attempt to set ourselves apart from others when we aren't that adequate, when we fall short. You only point a finger at someone else's failings or shortcomings when you don't want to draw attention to your own. You put others down to make yourself feel better. So when you stick your chest out proudly and say, "My people are *better* than yours!" you are really saying the opposite. You are allowing yourself (and the rest of us) through your divisiveness to be conquered.

I would like to carry this notion one step further. America is on the precipice of losing her greatness. Look at her economy. Look at her credibility. Look at the confidence or lack thereof other nations have in America. Some would say that water seeks its own level and the problems America is facing could be considered karma.

At one time, even when she was a hypocrite with her slavery and Jim Crow laws, Japanese internments, abuse of Chinese to build the railroads, and the decimation of the indigenous peoples that we call Indians, America stood for something. It was why black folks, who had to sit in the back of the bus and drink from a COLOREDS ONLY water fountain in America, could fly to another country and take up arms to fight for the United States.

We preached a mantra—united we stand, divided we fall. That notion of unity is part of the flag we fly; it's even written on our money.

Somehow all of that good old American feeling has left. And it has left us extremely vulnerable. Just like Rome, America is in an awful position where she could very well fall if she doesn't pull it together. America needs all of us—blacks, whites, Asians—who live here to stop dividing ourselves and separating ourselves with trivial, meaningless distinctions and to come together to make sure that we have a country to fight for in the future. America is slowly eating away at herself from the inside.

It won't be terrorism that will ultimately bring her down. It will be a lack of an identity born out of a desire to separate each of us from one another. Here's the deal whether you like it or not—we all came from the same place. Our DNA is all linked. We are *all* related. Sure, some individuals have more talent, higher IQs, stronger spirits.

But not one race of people is better than the next because we are all part of the same race—the human race.

FIVE

Stop Digging

Life is hard. It's even harder if you're stupid.

—ANONYMOUS

THIS CHAPTER IS not about black people, per se. But it's something that I've seen with a lot of people—myself included—and have to share. I call it compounding a fracture. When you're in a bad situation, sometimes in your haste to get out of it, you can make it worse—you compound the fracture.

Instead of sitting back, taking stock of where you are, and figuring out a sensible solution, you borrow money you can't pay back, you make bad deals with bad people, or you just make wrong moves that instead of helping your situation actually hurt it.

The primary reason why we do this is because we don't want to look bad. We don't want people to think that we don't have it all together. So we will beg, borrow, steal, and lie to cover up our mess. But it still stinks and people can still smell it.

In 1996, I was an ace reporter with the New York *Daily News,* had just got a seat on the prestigious editorial board. I was making $70,000 a year, driving a Saab convertible (limited edition, no less). From the outside, I had all of the trappings of a successful person. In reality I was broke. The repo man was looking for my car, I was months behind in my rent, and each month I owed about $200 more than I brought home.

The bottom came one payday when I went to the ATM to withdraw money to get me through the week and found my balance at zero. I had no money in my account. Nada. Zilch. Zippo! I had direct deposit of my paycheck, which was supposed to be in my account the evening before. I called the bank to find that not only was my account wiped out, but a hold was also on it—meaning any new money that came in would also be seized.

I was not only living paycheck to paycheck, I was also doing what millions of Americans do—paying my bills before my money was actually in my account. That week, I had mailed out my car payment, rent check, utilities bill, cell-phone bill, home-phone bill, a credit-card payment—all in *anticipation* of my check coming in that Friday. I didn't actually have the money. But I knew it was coming. Well, every single check I sent off bounced.

One of the creditors I owed had filed a judgment against me that I'd ignored. I compounded a fracture. Because of my neglect, thinking the creditor would never come after me, I put myself in a hole I could not see getting out of.

I thought about contacting an unsavory acquaintance of mine and asking him for a loan. But that loan came with strings that I was not willing to pluck. I even visited a lawyer to discuss the pros and cons of filing for bankruptcy. Bankruptcy seemed like the easy way out— wipe out all my debt and start over again. That would solve my current problem, but that bankruptcy would be on my credit history for ten years.

As I sat at my desk at the *Daily News*, contemplating my next move, I made a tough decision. I decided to stop digging.

The only way out of a hole that you have dug is to first stop digging. Then you must find a way to use the dirt in your hole to create a way to climb out. If it's not too deep, sometimes all you need is someone with a rope or a helping hand to help pull you out.

I sucked it up and accepted responsibility for my situation. I called my creditors and explained to them what had happened, and all of them accepted late payments and smaller payments than due. My patient landlord allowed me to get back on my feet, waiving an entire month so that I could catch up.

I didn't just stop digging, I created steps to get out. I spoke with my parents and asked them if I could move back in (that was one of the toughest decisions I made). I had been on my own since I graduated from college. I bought my first condo when I was twenty-three. A million thoughts ran through my head. At the top of that list was, what will my friends and colleagues think? Were any of them going to help me out of my hole? Probably not. But my parents were there for me.

Before hitting rock bottom, I had spent my twenties digging a hole. It took a failed marriage, a failed business, and losing my home, my luxury car, and all of my money before I finally stopped digging. Most people are smarter than I was. They don't wait to make a change. But some people are also still in that hole digging it deeper. After humbling myself and deciding to do something about my situation, I got a book deal and was able to get back on my feet financially. I was even able to save thanks to saving on rent and food by living with my parents (thanks, Mom, for the home-cooked meals, too).

What I learned from my failures (and there have been more since) is that things are never as bad as they seem. Sometimes just weathering the storm and enduring and pressing forward is all you need to do. Sometimes all you need to do is stop digging. Think of the worst thing that ever happened (excluding the tragic death of a loved one). If you did nothing to make it worse, does the pain feel the same over time? Nothing, if allowed to run its course, is as bad as it first seems.

When I started to look at setbacks and "failures" as blessings and opportunities from which to learn and grow, they became far easier to deal with. When I looked at the dirt in my hole as a stepping-stone to the next place, I figured a way out of that ditch onto solid land.

A parable about a donkey is popular but also appropriate. One day a farmer's donkey fell down into a well that the farmer had accidentally left uncovered. The animal cried piteously for hours as the farmer tried to figure out what to do. Finally, he decided the animal was old, and the well needed to be covered up anyway, so it just wasn't worth it to retrieve the donkey.

He invited all his neighbors to come over and help him. They all grabbed shovels and began to throw dirt into the well. At first, the donkey realized what was happening and cried horribly. Then, to everyone's amazement he quieted down.

A few shovel loads later, the farmer finally looked down into the well. He was astonished at what he saw. With each shovel of dirt that hit his back, the donkey was doing something amazing. He would shake it off and take a step up.

The farmer's neighbors continued to shovel dirt on top of the animal, and pretty soon, everyone was amazed as the donkey stepped up over the edge of the well and happily trotted off!

Life is going to shovel dirt on you. The trick to getting out of the well is to shake it off and take a step up.

When life isn't shoveling dirt on us, sometimes we dig our own holes. When you find yourself digging your own hole, stop digging, because the only difference between a ditch and a grave is a few feet.

SIX

Stop Devaluing Yourself

When you know you are of worth—not asking it, but knowing it—you walk into a room with a particular power. When you know you are of worth, you don't have to raise your voice, you don't have to become rude, you don't have to become vulgar; you just are. And you are like the sky is, as the air is, the same way water is wet. It doesn't have to protest.

—MAYA ANGELOU

I ALWAYS BELIEVED I could do anything I set my mind to doing. It's something my father hammered into me at a young age. "You're a Hunter!" he would proudly say, meaning there's nothing we can't do. But what my father failed to teach me was how to value myself. Not from a self-esteem standpoint, I think I got that one down pat. But from a marketplace standpoint.

While how you value yourself personally and how

you value yourself in the marketplace may directly be connected, it isn't necessarily so. Sometimes, it may just be experience.

When I wrote my first book in 1997, I had no clue what a writer should get. I didn't have any friends who had written books, and the few colleagues that I knew (Mike Lupica and Mike McAlary) were major columnists and commanded a big payday. This was my first book.

I hired an attorney, who was McAlary's agent, and I brought him in on a deal that I had already secured. Over lunch while doing a piece for the *Daily News,* I asked LL Cool J if he had ever thought about writing a book. He said he had. I asked him if he would want to do one with me, and he said yes. I didn't know him from Adam. We spent the day together for this feature article that I was going to write. I'm sure he had been interviewed by hundreds of reporters by this time, but perhaps none had ever asked him to write a book with them. I did.

I set up a meeting with a publisher, St. Martin's Press, with LL and his manager at the time. We secured the deal; LL got a rather hefty sum of money. What did I get? A measly amount of money that included bonuses. I was tempted to walk away from the deal because I felt that I was instrumental in making it all happen *and* I was going to write it. But the reality was, they could easily have got another writer at this point and left me out completely. So I sucked it up.

I don't regret that decision. But I do regret not arming myself with knowledge. To this day, the attorney jokes with me about how that book helped him put his daughter through college. He made more money on that deal than I did, which is a shame, right?

But shame on me! I should have had a collaboration deal *before* I even set up any meetings, spelling out what I would get. But I was just happy to be there.

Well, it's not enough to be just happy to be there. We have to get what we deserve in every situation. I made a couple more similar mistakes in my career that I look back on now, especially knowing what I know today, and I say, "What the heck!"

Value? What is it exactly? It's the price you place on your time and your talents. I love to teach, and I would probably do it for free. But I don't because I know that what I bring to the table few people can, and there is value that must be met.

When I was offered a full-time position at Hunter

College, I told them what I wanted to make. I had no clue what any of the other professors were making, so I asked for what I thought I was worth. About six months later, I had to sign off on my appointment letter, securing my position for the next year, and the young lady handling the forms accidentally gave me the form of a prominent professor who was full-time, tenured, and active in university matters. I accidentally signed his contract, which had his salary. That's when I noticed it wasn't mine. It was $25,000 less than what I was being paid!

I found out that my salary was above what many of the professors in my department were making. It had nothing to do with race. I was the only black female in my department. It was because I'd asked for what I thought I deserved.

I learned about value with the LL Cool J book and a few other experiences to never accept less than what I'm worth. People will pay you what you deserve, provided you are excellent at what you do—which is the other part of the equation.

You have to not just demand value for yourself, you have to demand it *from* yourself.

I have been a writer for more than twenty years,

and I still don't hesitate to hone my skills and bring on new challenges, because it's not enough to be just good enough. To get top dollar, you have to be the best. That's not necessarily about talent so much as it is about hard work and persistence. I read at least two books a month because it's in reading other peoples' works that I become a better writer. I've read *On Writing Well* by William Zinsser, *Eat, Shoots & Leaves* by Lynne Truss, and Walter Mosley's *This Year You Write Your Novel* because I want to continue to improve and sharpen my skills so that I can tell people with confidence, "I may be expensive, but you get what you pay for."

I have a friend who took a job at a major pharmaceutical company. She was offered a starting salary of $65,000 to handle all of the sales numbers in their marketing department. Her job required her to track all drugs, make sure they were shipped to the right locations, and track all returns. The company's entire revenue tracking was based on the work she did. If she was off by just a penny, it cost her company millions.

Her bosses stayed on her and continued to pile even their own work on her, and she would do it, like a workhorse.

A year after being hired, my friend learned that the

woman (a white woman) they originally offered the job to had turned it down because it was too much work. That woman was offered a starting salary of $80,000.

The $65,000 was more money than my friend had ever made. In her previous job she was making $45,000, so the $20,000 was a tremendous raise. But she had no clue that she could and should have asked for even more. The job was work-intensive, which the first woman knew immediately, and she knew that even $80,000 wouldn't be enough.

Since my friend left that position more than two years ago, that pharmaceutical company has still not found a replacement, and three people, including her former bosses, have had to pitch in to do the work that she did alone.

An unspoken (or perhaps it is spoken) rule in the white community is that their time is valuable. That they are worthy. I am generalizing because I am sure that plenty of white people don't value themselves, but the way they demand and command pay for their work does seem to be different. I got to see this as a boss a number of years ago.

When I started my first company in 1999, I got a nice investment from a group of men at Bear Stearns.

I set up my payroll and began to hire people. I had a small team of seven full-time employees and a handful of consultants. I asked everyone what he or she expected to be paid. One of the white women I hired boldly said, "Ninety-five thousand." She didn't flinch. She didn't waver. I had planned on paying myself only $90,000 because I didn't want to burden my company with a heavy payroll. I was thinking about offering her around $50,000.

But she asked for what she thought was right for her. It was an eye-opener because two of the black people that I was hiring, doing essentially the same job, requested $50,000! I ended up splitting the difference with the white woman and paying her $70,000.

I had a conversation with a guy who was once married to a celebrity figure. He is a businessman who worked for several years on Wall Street and watched this money game firsthand. He told me that black people often sell themselves short, especially in corporate America.

So, is it racism that blacks make seventy-four cents for every dollar a white person makes, or do we accept less? Do we value ourselves less? Do we feel that we're worth less?

I believe we do, for a number of reasons that can be tied to our history in America and throughout the world as chattel.

Whatever the reason, it's time we stop.

We owe it to ourselves and our progeny to get what we deserve from every situation—including relationships. Women (black, white, and others) stay in bad relationships because they don't think they deserve better.

I have been single for more than a decade. While it would be nice to be in a relationship with someone whom I can totally be myself with and share my life with, I haven't missed a beat in the happiness department. I learned through many years of pain and work on myself to really love the person I am, and in so doing, I can't accept less. I can't accept less in the workplace, I can't accept less in business, and I definitely can't do it in my personal life.

And neither should you!

SEVEN

Stop Disrespecting Your Money

*Whoever loves money, never has money enough;
whoever loves wealth is never satisfied with his
income. This too is meaningless.*

—ECCLESIASTES 5:10

A fool and his money are soon parted.

—PROVERB

I GOT A frantic call one afternoon from an author. He
said he was on the verge of losing his home and losing
his mind, and he asked me for advice. I didn't know him
well, but after asking a few pointed questions, I concluded that money (or lack of it) was not his problem.
My advice: Your life is out of order. Fix your life and
your money problems will straighten out.

In the meantime, he worked out a deal that would
pay him seven figures, including a hefty six-figure

amount within the week—virtually unheard of in publishing. I offered to help him get back on track. I put him in contact with a good friend whom I consider a financial guru. I gave him her number and told him that she was willing to work with him at a reduced rate. He said he would call. He never did.

Less than a month later, I got another frantic call from the same author.

"I'm desperate!"

I couldn't understand it. "What happened to that first check? You spent it *all*?"

The author talked about having to repay money he'd borrowed, and paying his back taxes and back mortgage, and now another home he owned was heading for foreclosure. He also needed money to "live."

After doing a bit of research, I found that this was his pattern. He would earn large sums of money and just as quickly spend it all. In his mind, there would always be that next deal. He never worried about budgeting or planning. He never set aside something for a rainy day. His rainy day came in the form of a hurricane, and he wasn't prepared for it.

Things do happen, but we also create the environment to not be prepared when they do.

For this author money was more like toilet paper,

something to use to take care of his business, but to be easily discarded and flushed away because there would always be another roll. He used money to create an image, for status, to be "the man" for everyone in his life—from paying tuition to buying homes and cars for others.

But he didn't respect his money. So it left him rather easily and often.

Just to break even, he had to work probably four times harder than someone else would to make a living. When the tide turned, he had no one to turn to.

I have heard a dozen stories just like this one. But this is the only one where I witnessed the lack of respect for money actually costing someone his or her life. The medical examiner will say it was heart failure. But I know it was brought on by the stress of not being able to pay his bills and hustling and running to try to stay ahead of the mess he made with his finances. It was too much. While he focused on chasing the ever-elusive dollar, he wasn't focused on the really important things in his life—such as his health.

How you handle your money indicates how your life is going. If you have chaos on your job and in your life, your money is guaranteed to be a mess.

If you are obese and out of control with your health,

I bet your money is out of control. You may have a lot of it, but it's probably not working for you, and you should have a whole lot more.

I know a woman who lived in my building. She had hit the lotto for a sizeable amount and bought a condo in cash and a brand-new vehicle. She made a decent living. Her only financial responsibilities were food, clothing, utilities, taxes on the condo, and insurance and gas for the car.

A few years ago before I moved, I got a frantic (why are these calls always frantic?) call from her in tears. She was on the verge of losing her condo. What?! Again, I was completely baffled. The taxes on her unit were about half of what mine were, and she had accrued several quarters of back taxes, interest, and other fees. I went down to city hall and paid her taxes because I couldn't see this woman losing her home. She promised to pay me back and even set up a payment plan.

A good friend of mine warned me that I would never see my money again.

"She's close to four hundred pounds and out of control. If she can't pay her taxes now, she won't be able to pay them again, and she definitely won't be able to pay you back. It's a pattern."

My friend, I hate to say it, was right. This woman has lost her condo, and I haven't heard from her since.

Money is an outward display of the discipline and standards of your life. If you don't care enough to take care of your health (which I will talk more about in the next chapter), how much energy will you put into making sure your finances are tight? Isn't your health more important?

If you can't seem to keep money or are always in some sort of financial disarray, look at your life.

This chapter is crucial to us as a people because as a group we spend, according to Target Market News, more than $700 billion. That is more than the GDP of Poland, Sweden, Greece, and Iran. We spend more than Syria, Luxembourg, Ecuador, and the Dominican Republic combined. We spend enough to own a nation, yet within America we lag behind just about every other group in income, home ownership, and business ownership.

As a group, we black people don't respect our money. We have made Tommy Hilfiger, Timberland, Lexus, Nike, and just about every liquor maker from Alizé to Courvoisier rich. How many of you own stock in any of those companies? How many of you have a stake in the companies that we have helped to prosper?

I've watched immigrant group after immigrant group come to this land of opportunity and make a way. Why? Because they value and respect their money. Everyone points to Jews and says, "They seem to own and control everything!" Don't hate the player or the game—learn the rules and play. If they pool their resources and build companies and industries and hire their people and promote their agendas, can't we?

We did it before in Rosewood, Florida, and the Greenwood section of Tulsa, Oklahoma. Those black-built communities were among the wealthiest in their respective states. Racism and terrorism brought both of those down, and perhaps fear keeps us from trying it again, but times are definitely different.

If we put that kind of energy into building up our communities, watch what would happen. It makes no sense that within any black neighborhood there are more "other"-owned businesses. It makes no sense because what that means is that the dollar spent in your community leaves your community (a fool and his money . . .). I'm not saying boycott the nail salon or the bodega, I'm saying we need to have our own.

Go to Chinatown—especially in New York. What do you see? Every single business owned by Chinese, and you see prosperity. I dare you to try to sell drugs or commit a crime in Chinatown. Watch what will happen. They police their own community, just as they do in Crown Heights, New York, and certain Italian neighborhoods. They work too hard building their community to allow anyone to come in and tear it down. They respect their money.

The other thing we must respect is work. Sure, we may have to work a little harder. Again, so what? Let's just do it. Because once it's done, we won't have to do it again. But if we sit around complaining about how unfair things are, it will never get done.

I have another wise friend who constantly quotes her grandmother, who used to say, "It's a poor mouse that has one hole."

What that means is that you have to have more than one stream of income or more than one way to pay for your things. If you're a writer and that's what you want to do, why not write while collecting a paycheck? Toni Morrison did that for a number of years before she finally finished *Beloved,* and I can name thousands of others who didn't give up their day job to pursue their dream.

Actually, I learned this mentality from my father, too. He worked as a parole officer for the State of New Jersey for sixteen years while he ran his corner store. He would get up at 5 a.m., open the store. Go from the store to the parole bureau. When he was done working, he would relieve his brother behind the counter and work until midnight. Every day. He didn't give up his day job, not even when he was raking in the big bucks. Why?

Because it's a poor mouse that has one hole, and he understood that he was a robbery, a fire, a lawsuit, away from being out of business. But that state job afforded him a consistent salary, a pension, and benefits. That's smart.

I get teased by some of my friends for having so many jobs. But given my personality, I know that I can't work for someone for long, so I have to have multiple streams of income.

On the flip side, many people look to their job as the end-all. Their job defines who they are, and as a result, when they "lose" that job, they are devastated and lost.

The story about that author who allowed his money problems to destroy him is, unfortunately, not an anomaly. In speaking with a publishing colleague, she told me that several authors have been contacting her in a panic over money.

"They are acting like we're their bank," she said.

But you need to be your own bank. You need to view

your money not as something that you earn, but rather something that works for you and something you must put to work.

You also have to tithe or give a portion of your money away to charity because of the law of giving and receiving. I don't know how or why it works, I just know that it does. I guess money is called currency for a reason. It has to flow. So you can't hoard it. But you also can't abuse it by spending it as if it will keep coming. Because chances are it won't.

Just watch nature. There is a season for everything. You plant, water, and fertilize, you watch the harvest grow, then you pick the harvest. There is a reason why half of the people who hit the lottery for millions are broke soon after.

If most of them had any respect for money or any concept about it, they wouldn't be wasting their precious dollars playing the lottery in the first place. People with a lottery mentality rely on luck, chance. They aren't working their money, and their money definitely isn't working for them. So when they finally hit (after wasting how many thousands?), they have no clue how to manage that money.

People who get these huge book, record, and movie deals fall into the same category. If you don't respect your money or take the time to learn how to respect it, it will soon leave you. I can write pages about the number of record-label executives and recording artists, television and movie stars, who have gone broke. It is a culture and a mentality.

Another reason so many lottery winners, rappers, singers, authors, etc., end up broke is that they feel compelled to take care of everyone. Generosity is a simple act of kindness or giving more than is expected or necessary. You can be generous with your time, you can be generous with your knowledge, and you can certainly be generous with your money. But the rule of thumb here is to take care of home first. You cannot go out and clean somebody's house and come home to roaches and rats. Not cool.

I see people get a windfall (even an income-tax return) and they decide they're going to splurge, throw a party, go out to eat, buy an outfit, instead of getting out of debt or saving for a rainy day. I've seen people get large sums and decide they're going to buy someone (or themselves) a house or a car or some other big-ticket item that requires a whole lot more than the asking price. (When you factor in insurance, maintenance costs, taxes, the expenses can keep climbing.)

People go out and get the luxury car. While they can afford the list price, they may not be able to afford all that comes with that luxury car. I'm no financial expert, this is just common sense (and actually a little bit of experience, having owned more than ten cars in my lifetime).

My only goal here is to get you to respect your money (yourself and your legacy).

Napoleon Hill wrote a book in 1937 entitled *Think and Grow Rich.* My father had an old, dog-eared copy that he got in college, which I borrowed. I, in turn, bought a deluxe edition for my brother's twenty-fifth birthday, and I recommend it to anyone who will listen.

Think and Grow Rich lays down principles that will help you think about yourself and how you view money and what money really means and does. You need to understand this currency to master it.

After you get your foundation, you build on it with *The Automatic Millionaire* by David Bach, and Robert Kiyosaki's first book, *Rich Dad, Poor Dad*, and any Suze Orman book.

But your journey to being truly wealthy starts with your taking the first step.

EIGHT

Stop Being Fat!

Whoever hears of fat men heading a riot, or herding together in turbulent mobs? No—no, [it's] your lean, hungry men who are continually worrying society, and setting the whole community by the ears.

—WASHINGTON IRVING

ACCORDING TO THE U.S. Office of Minority Health, about four out of five African-American women are either overweight or obese. Four out of five! From 2003 to 2006, African-American women were 70 percent more likely to be obese than white women.

And it's getting worse each year.

But you don't need the statistics; all you need to do is look around. Or in the mirror. I go to the gym three times a week and it's packed—with mostly white women. They drop off their kids at day care at the gym, then are in aerobics class, spin class, on the treadmills, on the bikes, in the pool. They are there. We are not.

Now I love to eat. I love being here and being healthy more than food. But I wasn't always like that. I battled weight almost my entire life. But I got a scare (actually two) a number of years ago. I had been having pains in my stomach for more than a year. I thought it was gas. It all exploded one night at 2 a.m. I got violently ill and my stomach hurt so badly that I was rushed to the hospital and I wished to die. Seriously. I would have preferred death.

My gallbladder had so many stones that it was infected. They removed it. But they never told me why or how it happened. I went online and discovered that gallbladder issues derive from a high-fat diet. Every Sunday, I would stop by KFC for chicken strips and their thick-cut fries. It was my reward for what I felt was working hard during the week. And it wasn't just KFC. It was the grits, the fried whiting, the ___ (fill in the blank). I was eating myself to death.

A couple of years after that, I had a lump in my breast. Of course, it was unnerving. I had a mammography and discovered that I had a cyst. This time the doctor told me if I didn't change my diet, I could expect more of the same—and worse.

I had a decision to make: be "happy" eating what I

wanted, or change the way I ate and thought about food and my health. I decided to change. No more white flour, white sugar, white rice. No more saturated fats. I dropped close to forty pounds, and the cyst magically disappeared.

I still love to eat (especially Toll House chocolate-chip cookies), and I hate working out, I really do. But I hate being a statistic more.

How about you?

We make excuses. "I'm just big-boned." I tried that one and my doctor took an X-ray and showed me that not only was I *not* big-boned, but my bone structure was actually quite delicate.

"It's in my genes. I can't help it, fat runs in my family." Yep. My grandmother and "all of the women on my father's side of the family are fat," I would say. Guess what: we all ate the same way. Poor eating habits may run in your family, but being fat does not. And even if you are predisposed to holding weight, is that any excuse not to try to lose it?

"It costs too much money to eat healthy."

Okay, that may be true. Fresh fruits and vegetables are more expensive. But if you can drop $20 a week on your nails and another $40–$50 on your hair, you can certainly find it in your budget to shop for food that will extend your health and your life.

"I'm not fat, I'm big, bold, and beautiful." Thanks, Mo'Nique, for that one! No, you're fat! The sooner we admit it, the sooner we will be working toward fixing it. Sure, you must love yourself no matter what, but if your body is your temple, what God are you praying to?

Don't get me started with the church crowd on this. Those church dinners have contributed more to obesity in the black community than anything else.

I will offer this: If you are made in the image of God, are you really representing the Almighty? If your mission is to bring people to the Lord, are you being a good ambassador? To be obese is to lack self-control, discipline, and to not truly love yourself. You cannot be a good Christian and be obese.

We also have to stop setting bad examples for our children.

We have to empower ourselves and stop allowing retailers and advertisers to infect our neighborhoods with their poisons.

Please take a drive through a white neighborhood (preferably during the day, I don't want anyone getting pulled over for driving while black). Let me know how many fast-food restaurants are in middle-class, white neighborhoods.

Where I used to live in Orange, New Jersey, in a two-block radius from Central Avenue were a Popeyes, a Wendy's, a KFC, and a McDonald's, and if you went a couple blocks farther toward South Orange, there was a White Castle. Harlem? Forget about it. Sure they have a Starbucks now, but how many Kansas Fried Chickens, Mama's Fried Chickens, and some other fried chicken joints are there, not to mention the other brand-name fast-food restaurants?

(Oh, yeah, and what about the liquor stores? One stretch in Harlem has a liquor store, church, liquor store, church, liquor store . . . you get the picture.)

And advertising? Please go back to that white neighborhood (during the daytime, of course). Tell me how many beer and cigarette ads there are.

This part is a function of a lack of ownership, which I deal with in another chapter. Since we don't own the stores in our neighborhood, then it goes that we don't own the billboard space. But there is another issue.

White folks won't allow crap in their neighborhoods that will infect their children. They don't just allow things to be done to them. They show up at council meetings. They're vocal.

We could argue that this is more of a class issue than a race issue because you don't see those ads in middle-class black neighborhoods, either. But it still doesn't explain why blacks are almost two times more obese than whites collectively. Even middle-class and wealthy blacks. It's something we must seriously consider.

This isn't about vanity. This is about health.

We have to stop eating so much and eating so much of the wrong things. Our diet and obesity are gateways to so many other diseases, of which blacks suffer more than whites.

In addition to leading the nation (and the world) in the obesity category, blacks also lead the nation in just about every other category:

- Compared to any other group, black women are more likely to get heart disease and die from it.
- African-American men are at least 50 percent more likely to develop lung cancer than white men.
- African-American men are twice as likely to be diagnosed with prostate cancer as white men.
- Blacks lead all races in diabetes cases, and our death rate from the disease is 40 percent higher than for any other race.

- According to the Centers for Disease Control, more than 40 percent of blacks over the age of twenty have hypertension, and 80 percent of black people over the age of forty-five have high blood pressure.

We also lead the nation in new AIDS cases and in homicide-related deaths, which while have nothing to do with diet, certainly have everything to do with a lack of love of self.

While I'm on this issue of health, let's throw liquor into the mix.

I set up a business meeting one time in Brooklyn. It was my first meeting with Teddy Vann, and we were discussing this sports marketing idea I had. I invited him to this beautiful restaurant overlooking the East River near the Brooklyn Bridge. I was in my twenties and thought I was hot stuff. I ordered a cosmopolitan or some such chic drink, and Teddy just shook his head at me. He had never met me before but he was bold enough to say, "Young lady, why are you ordering a drink?"

I was puzzled. I mean, doesn't everyone drink at business meetings?

"You never drink while conducting business," he said, not waiting for me to respond. "You need to be clear and sober at all times when talking business. They used alcohol to get the Indians, and do you see any te-pees around?"

I had never thought about it. But it made perfect sense. I have since given up liquor altogether. I don't need it. I should be able to function and be relaxed and myself without a narcotic.

I have an artist friend who claims she cannot create without smoking weed. It's a cop-out and an excuse.

Food, liquor, drugs, are crutches, they are weak props. They allow you to hide and run and never fully develop.

We must stop all of it. If we don't, it will stop us.

NINE

Stop Letting People Destroy
Our Images

WHEN BOB JOHNSON launched BET (Black Entertainment Television) in 1980, the hope was that black people would have a network of their own to showcase the ample talents of black screenwriters, moviemakers, actors, singers, and other entertainers. It was going to be the black answer to MTV.

What we got was a network full of rap and R&B videos that showcased booty-shaking, gun-toting, and weed-smoking, perpetuating every negative stereotype of blackness that no white network would dare to air. If BET were run by whites, Al Sharpton, Jesse Jackson, and a host of other civil rights activists would have picketed, marched, and called for a boycott.

Amos and Andy were more empowering than BET.

Yet, not only didn't blacks boycott, we viewed the network in large numbers—large enough for founder Bob Johnson to net a billion-dollar-plus profit when he sold out to Viacom.

Good for him. Bad for us. But I can't blame Johnson. He was a businessman. Just because he was black didn't mean he was supposed to care about his people and their images. He was in it to make a buck and he did. We, as a community, however, bore a responsibility to let him know that his brand of business was not welcome. We failed to do our job. We live in a capitalist society. It's supply and demand. What we told Bob Johnson and now Viacom is that we like the crap that they produce.

The problem is that too many of us don't do or say anything because we don't see the harm. Or we think, "It's better to have a BET than to have nothing."

Well, think again!

Bob Johnson single-handedly did what no white man could—destroy an entire generation of black youth through negative, misogynistic, and violent images bombarded daily. No white person could have got away with that without hearing from the likes of Al Sharpton. But we rewarded Bob Johnson with silence and support. He sold BET (he was a sellout in more ways than one) for a billion-dollars-plus profit. Yes, the establishment will reward those among us who do their dirty work (see Larry Elder, Jesse Lee Peterson, Ward Connerly, Clarence Thomas . . . among others).

In fact, since Viacom took over BET, I was told by several high-level executives of an edict about the kinds of things they will never allow on the air—meaning Viacom cares more about the images they are projecting of black people than the black man who started the network.

Oprah Winfrey relays a story of her first trip to Africa and how when she got off the airplane, she was greeted by "What's up, my nigga!" from one of the workers at the airport. Where did he get the notion that greeting Ms. Winfrey in that manner would be acceptable? Probably from a rap video (or a bombardment of rap videos).

Images—especially visual images—matter. You are what you eat, they say. I will take that one step further. You are what you view and what you read. Your television, movie, and reading diet define you perhaps more than anything else. These images can either reinforce the deep-seated self-hatred many of us carry as a remnant of slavery, or they can break down the stereo-types and create a whole new reality.

But we have to be proactive.

For years we complained about the stealing of our music. Then along comes Berry Gordy, who not only provided a platform for our artists to have a voice and be part of the business, but also trained and coached these artists in how to act, perform, and build the right image for not just themselves, but the entire black community.

He cared. And it showed.

Bill Cosby, to whom I devoted an entire chapter, had a tremendous impact not just on black culture, but white culture as well. Through television, he showed black success. He was a doctor, married to a lawyer, raising five children, who were all expected to attend college and excel in life. While America would have us believe that Florida and James Evans were the model black family, the Cosbys were more in line with my up-bringing. I could relate. For those who couldn't relate, they could aspire.

A college friend of mine, Kevin Mason, who grew up in Newark, New Jersey, without a father in his home, talks poignantly about how Bill Cosby taught him to be a father. Watching that show taught him the values he now uses to raise his own children. He learned that from a television show because his daddy wasn't there to teach him. So how important are images? Very!

That said, when we allow others to define who we are and we say nothing, then we can't be mad when we travel around the world and people treat us like niggers, because those are the images we allow the world to see when we produce music videos and those ghetto *Flavor of Love* and *I Love New York* (and the myriad spin-offs that followed) television shows where all people see is cussing, fighting, bad grammar, and fornication. That's who we are to the world because when given an opportunity to show something different, we offer up BET.

CNN, the cable news outlet, released a clever series during the 2008 presidential election called *Black in America*.

I mean what the . . . is that? When do we hold up an entire group like that for examination? If they were going to do a series, why not cover every group? No, they followed that the next year with *Black in America 2*, with the excuse that this time instead of focusing on all of the negative statistics (the crime rate, drug use, fatherlessness, in our community), they would focus on the success stories. But the damage was done.

Ironically, CNN did a series on religious fanatics reported by the powerful Christiane Amanpour, and they took the trouble to include Muslims, Jews, and Christians. Each group got their turn. While they produced *Latino in America* in October 2009, there hasn't been an *Asian in America*, a *White in America* series to follow *Black in America*. Why?

The bigger why is, why did we allow it? We made *Black in America*, according to CNN itself, "the most watched cable series in history."

We allow ourselves to be examined and held up for discussion, we even participate without ever considering how this plays out. You don't see any other group sitting back and taking that. (And for the record, I consider Latinos to be black, so *Latino in America* is more of the same.)

The mammy, the pickaninny, the coon, the sambo, the uncle: Well into the middle of the twentieth century, these were the most popular depictions of black Americans. By 1941, (these images) permeated American culture. These are the images that decorated our homes, that served and amused and made us laugh. Taken for granted, they worked their way into the mainstream of American life. Of ethnic caricatures in America, these have been the most enduring. Today there is little doubt that they shape the most gut-level feelings about race.

—from Marlon Riggs's documentary,

　　Ethnic Notions, narrated by Esther Rolle

In the 1820s, T. D. Rice brought his happy sambo, mockery of blacks to theaters in America. This white comedian would don blackface and dance and coon around the stage as a character that became known as Jim Crow. He was an instant hit. And he set off what would be the rave in America—the blackface minstrel shows.

According to *Ethnic Notions,* this image came to define black people.

"But what was bought by the majority of the people in Ohio, and the Louisiana Territory, and in, along the Erie Canal, was that this was a true image. And it was a devastating image. People in small towns who had never seen blacks, (who) suddenly saw Rice, bought that as a black image."

When filmmaking began, the assault on the black image was heightened. *Birth of a Nation,* praised as one of the best films ever made is a Ku Klux Klan–inspired movie depicting blacks as savage, childlike and inhuman beings that needed to be stopped and controlled. The end of slavery was the end of civilization, the film argues, and white knights on horses were needed to restore order and protect the white woman from the black savage.

In *Birth of a Nation* you will see every character that would become the formula and foundation for how blacks would be depicted in movies to come, according to *Toms, Coons, Mulattoes, Mammies & Bucks* by Donald Bogle.

There was the mammy who, according to Bogle's book, was an asexual, loud, but obedient, loyal (to massa), fat, dark-skinned woman. Hattie McDaniel became the first black woman to win an Oscar playing . . . mammy!

There was the coon, a grown man acting like a child, and demonstratively foolish, a clown (meant to prove that blacks did not have the mental capacity to be equal to whites). There was the Uncle Tom. We slap that label erroneously on people when we want to say they are "selling out" the race. But Uncle Tom was merely an elderly, very religious, docile, emasculated and subservient man. More than a sell-out, he was a good Negro who could be trusted (by whites).

There was the pickaninny, a wild, untamed child, a small beast, often depicted in the woods or fields being chased. The pickaninny would always have wild, unruly hair so he or she would look like a small animal without any human value or qualities. Then there was the buck, a strong, hypersexual black man. He was always depicted as violent and a threat (physically and sexually) to the white woman. You can throw in the tragic mulatto and you have the range of black folks in America.

That was the foundation of the black image in film from its inception. So as you sit in the theater watching movies today, can you pick out any of those characters? Does Madea or Martin Lawrence's Big Momma fit a bill? Are they perpetuating the very images that were created to keep us in a certain place in society? Do you plunk down money and cosign your own assassination? Well, you should stop! And more than that, we should hold our own filmmakers accountable.

We complain about the images of us in movies, yet when we get an opportunity to produce movies, what do we put out: *Soul Plane*? And, sorry, I love your heart, Tyler Perry, but you're part of the problem. *Meet the Browns*? Are you serious? *House of Payne*? Please, come on!

Tyler Perry has amassed enough wealth to produce quality, excellent cinematic pieces. He no longer has to rush to production, throw together a movie, throw in Madea flopping around like a coon, and think that's enough. It's not enough.

Kudos to Spike Lee, who keeps pushing the envelope and continues to take his craft to the next level. Would you even know that *Miracle at St. Anna* was a "black" movie by Spike Lee? It wasn't a black movie, and that's the point.

We didn't make that well-done movie number one at the box office, but we make sure that every one of Tyler Perry's movies is? We should definitely support our own, but we must also press each other to be excellent. We shouldn't accept *Meet the Browns* and reward Tyler with a number one movie the next time out. If he's not going to uphold his end of the bargain, we must withhold our support and dough.

We complain about the disparity of power in the media, and there is. How many black talk show hosts are there on cable news television? Blacks supposedly make up 12.5 percent of the population, but represent only 4 percent of the newsroom reporters across the country. So if we get in the door, please represent. Your black behind is there to be black—make sure you make a difference in how we're presented. Be loud and vocal and public when you get pushed back because it's important.

Instead, we get in the door and give the world Madea and BET.

We want to prove so much that we aren't biased that we go in the opposite direction (hello, Clarence Thomas). We fight so hard against the stereotypes about us that we don't fight for our causes.

In 1999, the *Daily News* won a Pulitzer Prize for its editorial series to save the world-famous Apollo Theatre. The series took off after a tour and the questions it provoked: "Why is this landmark in such disarray? Don't they have a TV show? Why does it look so bad?" After some digging, we found out that those black folks looking after this Harlem institution were actually using it and not giving back.

But the Pulitzer would never have come about had I not been there. I was in on those meetings with

Sharpton and Wyatt T. Walker because, of course, the cries of racism were raging because the *Daily News*, which does have a racist history, was "attacking" the Apollo. No, we were saving the Apollo, and I was able to articulate that to our black leaders.

There were no marches or picketing of the *News* after that.

The Apollo has a new board, it got a face-lift, and it's being watched over by Time Warner.

Sometimes the ones we have to protect ourselves from are those who look like us.

We can't let others (even other blacks) put images out into the world that show us in a negative light. We have to fight back, speak out, and say, "Stop!"

TEN

Stop Being Niggardly

Niggardly, adj. (often offensive): not generous, stingy. Meager. Scanty. Cheap.

NOW WHAT DOES all that I've written so far have to do with being niggardly? I'm glad you asked. Oftentimes when we start a business or make any major decisions in our lives, we do it in a niggardly manner, meaning we cheat ourselves. We're stingy with us. We don't properly plan, we don't gather the information we need, we think small, and we execute at an even smaller level.

I could easily have started a publishing house by printing up some books for people and putting them out into the marketplace. I might even have sold a few. But would that model ever compete with what I envisioned, which was to have a house that long after I was gone would be mentioned in the same breath as Simon & Schuster and Random House?

To be big, you have to think big.

Simon & Schuster was founded by Richard Simon and Max Schuster, two guys who started publishing crossword puzzles. There was Nelson Doubleday and Henry Holt and Alfred Knopf.

These men all had a vision to start a publishing house, and they did it. But they had help. All of them. They had friends and family—people who looked like them—who helped fund their dream.

What most frustrated me about starting my publishing house was that despite so many resources—Earl Graves, Ed Lewis, and a dozen or so multimillionaire Wall Street types (who hadn't lost their shirt when the markets crashed)—no one saw value in my venture. I told them all what I was doing—not what I was planning to do, but what I was actually doing—and not one offered to help. Not one.

I thought it was interesting considering that not a single black major book-publishing house was in the marketplace. You would think someone would at least offer his or her business expertise. Not one.

Black folks have often been accused of being crabs in a barrel. As soon as one tries to get out, the ones at the bottom grab on, making sure that the one that is almost out doesn't make it to freedom. And those who make it out seem to try to shut the lid to make sure the rest stay in their place.

Niggardly.

Beyond business, people are stingy with themselves and the things around them.

I tithe. I understand it was a law from the Old Testament and many Christians today don't think that it's still relevant. I don't tithe to be legalistic. I tithe because giving opens up my world. Whether I tithe 10 percent to my church or I use my offerings to help buy medicine for someone suffering from cancer who doesn't have health insurance or I help put a kid through school, the reward of that giving is inexplicable.

During one of the most trying periods of my life, I made a commitment to tithe. The way I looked at it, if God allowed me to make whatever I made and all He asked for was 10 percent, then that was the least I could do. I faithfully tithed, even though, as I looked at my bank account at times, it made no sense.

During this period I was offered a book deal to do Mason Betha's story. It was right on time, because I don't think I could have covered my bills another month. With that check, I paid off my car and freed myself from some debt. I believe that it was my spirit of giving, even when money was tight, that opened me up to also receive opportunities from others.

I have a friend who has an aunt who always seems to have money. She was the wealthy one in a poor family, and oftentimes her family would turn to her when they needed something. She was so stingy that she rarely, if ever, lent or gave money to her family, even when in need. When she did lend, which was rare, she tortured the borrowers to the point that they wished they had never borrowed from her.

My friend was in her final year of school and needed $1,200 for tuition to remain registered. She would have been the first person in the family to graduate from college, and her mother didn't have the money. They scraped together $700 and went to the aunt for the final $500. The aunt said no.

Fast-forward fifteen years, and that same aunt had a stroke and had to depend on those same family members to take care of her. Guess what? Nobody was there for her. Not her children. Not her grandchildren. My friend visits her aunt from time to time and provides her with the only source of comfort in her life.

There are practical reasons to not be stingy, and it's not just about money. You can be stingy with yourself and suffer as well.

I have another friend, Ted, who was raised one of ten in a family with little money.

"Food was scarce," he said. "We couldn't wait for holidays because then we would be sure of getting something to eat. Some of us would hide our food so that we would make sure to have some."

Fast-forward into adulthood. Ted was hanging with one of his friends. They would often go to dinner, and his friend would offer him food off his plate every time. Every time Ted would accept.

"One time, after about a year of hanging out, my friend finally said something to me," Ted said. "He asked me why I had never offered him anything off of my plate. I never thought about it. I guess, considering my upbringing of never having enough, it never dawned on me to offer anyone food. I'm glad he said something and brought it to my attention because I've never let that happen again."

For Ted, not offering food was a by-product of growing up in lack, in a niggardly state. If his friend were a different person, he could simply have deemed Ted selfish. But in realizing this and changing, Ted enjoys much better relationships with his friends.

I sponsored a golfer in 2008. I met him in Florida on a golf course where he worked fixing carts. In his spare time, he would give lessons for free and for small change. The course stopped him from doing so because they said he was taking money away from their real pros.

I decided that I would help him get his pro card so that he could give all of the lessons he wanted and get the money he deserved. I discovered that this man was really good, and I had a vision of his becoming a champion on the senior tour. Mr. James was sixty-eight years old and had while growing up in Alabama learned to play golf with a makeshift club made from an old hanger and some duct tape. He had caddied for some of the best golfers in the country and had played with and beaten the likes of Jim Thorpe. Mr. James was a modern Bagger Vance. While I had a grand vision for him, he didn't have one for himself.

I gave him $2,500, which was the amount he needed to attend qualifying school to get onto the tour, or at the very least get his pro card so that he could teach. Instead, he used the money to play in small tournaments.

He didn't think he was ready for Q school and wanted to "warm up" in a few local tournaments. The first tournament in which he played, he won. He got $5,000. Under our agreement, I was entitled to my investment back. He cried broke and said he needed the money.

No problem. He was scheduled to be in two more tournaments, which I was certain he would win. I would get my money back, and he would have enough to enter Q school and start his journey toward making history as the oldest person to qualify for the pro tour.

He came in second in the next tournament, bagging $3,000. Mr. James dropped out of the next tournament because he was angry that they lowered his handicap, meaning he wouldn't have as much of an advantage. Well, that's what happens when you play well and win. Instead of being energized by his success, it seemed to scare him. He wouldn't play in any more tournaments and had within two months spent all of his earnings.

Not only did Mr. James not end up on the senior tour, he never got his pro card to give lessons, and he spent every dime he won on things that didn't enrich his life. He didn't put a down payment on a home to move out of the ghetto. He didn't get his teeth fixed (he had several missing in the front), which would have given him more confidence to interact with people. He didn't get rid of his broken-down hoopty for a better, more reliable car. He was no better off because he was not only niggardly with himself—having a stingy view of his future—he was also niggardly with me, not honoring our agreement and following through with what he'd said he was committed to doing.

Today, Mr. James is worse off than when I met him. The golf course cut down on his hours (he could have replaced that income by giving lessons), his car is constantly in the shop (requiring money and his taking days off to get it fixed), and he tasted success and lost it (which often is more difficult to deal with than having never tasted success at all).

Being niggardly or cheap or stingy guarantees you will always be in lack. You may keep your money, but I bet you will have shorts in other areas of your life.

So stop being niggardly! Stop cheating yourself out of the blessings you are supposed to have by focusing on the things you don't have, by looking at what others have and are doing instead of being excellent and following your own path and purpose.

With that message, I hand these pages over to a

woman I have grown to respect immensely for her wisdom and insight.

The next section of this book is devoted to celebrating the power of black people. That's how I look at it. It's an action plan to being the best we can be as a group. This is important not as some black-power excursion, but because our nation is made up of many groups of people—some who willingly came to this country for a better life, and others who came here in shackles—who want the American Dream.

Each of us, from a variety of racial and ethnic backgrounds, can have this by focusing first on being the best we can be individually. Once we take care of home, we can focus on contributing to the greatness of the country.

I look at black America as home, and we have some housecleaning to do. If we individually follow the simple rules given to us by Nannie Helen Burroughs, we will be a whole lot closer collectively to realizing that dream.

Twelve Things the Negro Must Do

by Nannie Helen Burroughs

(with commentary by Karen Hunter)

Who Is Nannie Helen Burroughs?

I CAME ACROSS Nannie Helen Burroughs by accident in 2002. Actually, a listener of my morning talk-radio show sent me her essay *Twelve Things the Negro Must Do*. What struck me initially was how bold her statements were. She wrote this in the 1890s when not just blacks, but women, had no voice. Here she was telling it like it is, saying the things that would ultimately give her people power—not over anyone, but power over themselves and their own lives.

What Burroughs understood more than a hundred years ago, which many people still don't get, is that freedom is not something someone can deny you. True freedom and true success and prosperity are generated within a people. Having standards and a commitment to excellence can defy any attempt to discredit or discriminate.

What Burroughs understood more than a hundred years ago is that if a group committed themselves to some simple truths and living those out, they wouldn't need anyone. If they could be self-sufficient and self-reliant, then even a racist America, one bent on separating and dividing, would have no choice but to acknowledge them or let them be.

So Burroughs, born in 1879 in Orange, Virginia, the eldest daughter of John and Jennie Burroughs, both born into slavery, was very much free. She learned that education—knowledge—was power. After the death of her father, her mother took Burroughs and her sister to Washington, D.C.

She graduated from high school with honors in 1896 and received an honorary masters from Eckstein-Norton University in Kentucky. She wanted to become a teacher but was denied a position by the board of education in the District of Columbia.

Instead of wallowing in self-pity, she used the power of words to empower others. Burroughs moved to Philadelphia and became associate editor of a Baptist newspaper, the *Christian Banner*. She moved back to D.C., more educated and more prepared. She expected to get an appointment this time after receiving high ratings on her civil service exam. Again she experienced disappointment when she was told there were no jobs for a "colored girl."

Did she cry racism? Did she complain and whine about the white man keeping her down? Did she let the exclusion keep her from her goal?

No.

She decided to start her own school, which allowed her to have a greater impact on a larger number of students.

"My school would give all sorts of girls a fair chance," she would say.

Burroughs didn't have much money, but she had heart and drive. She took a job as an office-building janitor and later took a position as a bookkeeper for a manufacturing company. She then accepted a position in Louisville, Kentucky, as a secretary for the Foreign Mission Board of the National Baptist Convention. She saved enough to open in the early 1900s the Women's Industrial Club, which offered short-term lodging to black women and taught them basic domestic skills. The organization also provided moderate-cost lunches for downtown office workers.

Later Burroughs started to hold classes, for ten cents a week, for club members majoring in business. In 1907, with the support of the National Baptist Convention, Burroughs began coordinating building plans for the National Trade and Professional School for Women and Girls, located in Washington, D.C.—the very city that had denied her access to their classrooms.

Burroughs's school opened its doors in 1909 with her as president. Her motto: "We specialize in the wholly impossible."

The wholly impossible!

Burroughs understood that through education, desire, faith, and sheer will, all things *were* possible. Her curriculum was designed to emphasize practical as well as professional skills. Her students were taught to be self-sufficient wage earners as well as "expert homemakers." She believed her duty was to see that an industrial and a classical education be simultaneously attained.

She demanded excellence. It was said that grammatical errors were physically painful to her, and she required courses on a high school and a junior college level to develop her students' language skills.

The National Trade and Professional School also maintained a close connection between education and religion. Its creed, stressed by Burroughs, consisted of the three B's: "The Bible, the bath, the broom—clean life, clean body, clean house."

Burroughs also understood that for people to have a real future, they must understand from whence they came. History—black history—was another foundational piece stressed by Burroughs at her school.

Today, Burroughs is part of history. In 1964, the National Trade and Professional School was renamed Nannie Burroughs School. In 1975, the then mayor of D.C., Walter E. Washington, proclaimed May 10 to be Nannie Helen Burroughs Day in the District of Columbia.

Burroughs died in 1961, but what she accomplished and her words of wisdom live on. With respect and a deep, abiding sense of history I give you *Twelve Things the Negro Must Do.*

Let's honor Nannie Helen Burroughs by making her words become flesh by incorporating them into our daily lives.

ONE

The Negro Must Learn to Put First Things First. The First Things Are: Education; Development of Character Traits; a Trade and Home Ownership

BURROUGHS

The Negro puts too much of his earning in clothes, in food, in show, and in having what he calls "a good time."

Dr. Kelly Miller said, "The Negro buys what he *wants* and begs for what he needs." Too true!

HUNTER

This first Burroughs missive almost needs no commentary. She incorporates so much in one sentence. Putting first things first. Some could say put God first (well, that goes without saying and we will definitely get to that). But what I think Burroughs was really getting at is to lay your foundation. You don't build a home without pouring the foundation. The deeper the foundation is poured, the more sturdy the house will be.

I believe the foundation in this case is education. But not just reading, writing, and arithmetic. Too many things are learned in school that you never need or use. So many things that are never taught in school you must absolutely learn. Two of the things are how to manage your money and how to manage yourself.

Building your wealth and building your character will ensure that your life is sturdy. MLK said, "Intelligence plus character—that is the goal of true education."

It used to be a running joke about the number of Lexus and Mercedes cars, flat-screen TVs, and other luxury items in the projects. But it really isn't funny. It's sad that instead of putting money into home ownership, savings, and education, people with limited funds buy and spend beyond their means.

In 2008, when the bottom fell out of the economy, this hit the African-American community particularly hard. When unemployment soared at the beginning of

2009, who lost their jobs first? When foreclosures went up over 80 percent over the previous two years, who was losing their homes?

A popular money scribe used to say, "If it's on your ass, it's not an asset."

I had a conversation once with a man who had a seat on the New York Stock Exchange. He was one of the first black men to have such a position. I asked him why there weren't more blacks with aspirations to own a home or to own a seat on the stock exchange. He told me, "Perhaps it's our history with being owned that turns us off to the notion of ownership."

I'm not buying that. I believe that ignorance is what keeps us from the golden prizes and being at the center of the money game.

I was fortunate. My father owned a corner store in Newark, New Jersey, for eighteen years. Every night after he came home from closing the store, he would count his money and reconcile his books. He would put some money away for me, and every week when he did, he would show me my savings book (this was before electronic banking). I would often go to the bank with him to make the deposits. He would even have me rolling the quarters, dimes, nickels, and pennies he received at his store. I enjoyed that, and it introduced me to the value of money. It taught me to respect money and have a healthy understanding of its power.

How many parents do that for their children? So if you're in a household where your parents are constantly robbing Peter to pay Paul, and living paycheck to paycheck, and following their instant-gratification jones by buying whatever they want even if they can't afford it, what do you think will be your experience?

My father's father owned that same corner store, which my father took over after my grandfather died. My grandfather didn't have a formal education in running a business, and my father became the first in his family to graduate from college, with a degree in accounting and business. He took the foundation his father started and built upon it.

With the knowledge I grew up with, I launched several businesses and even took it one step further—with investors and major contracts with Fortune 500 companies.

One of the best things about America (and there are quite a few great things about our nation) is that it is a capitalist society. That means if you know how to make money, save money, and utilize money, you can do absolutely anything you want. While in many arenas people may want to hold you back because of your race, or your gender or whatever, the color green always speaks louder than any of that.

Ask Oprah Winfrey. And Earl Graves. Ask Robert Johnson. Ask Barack Obama. Obama overcame the race thing because he raised more money than any other candidate in history. Money talks and it can walk you anywhere—even into the White House.

So when Burroughs talks about putting first things first, she is saying so much more. You don't successfully get anywhere in this world without knowing, without educating yourself. There are no excuses.

Famed playwright August Wilson dropped out of school at an early age. But he took himself to the library every single day, soaking up as much knowledge as he could. He read everything he could get his hands on and got his GED after studying in the library. He went on to be one of the most successful playwrights from our community.

He understood the value of a good education and

developing character. His hard work and uncompromising drive led him to great success and wealth.

August Wilson proved that it is never too late to put first things first.

He is just one example. Thousands and thousands more are out there.

TWO

The Negro Must Stop Expecting God and White Folk to Do for Him What He Can Do for Himself

BURROUGHS

It is the "Divine Plan" that the strong shall help the weak, but even God does not do for man what man can do for himself. The Negro will have to do exactly what Jesus told the man (in John 5:8) to do—carry his own load—"Take up your bed and walk."

HUNTER

I received an e-mail early in 2009 from the friend of a man who was supposed to be this incredible writer. She said he'd written this great book but no one would help him get it published.

Immediately, I had a problem with this e-mail. For one, if the man was so hard-pressed to get his book published, he would have reached out to me directly. (Note: never send someone else to do your bidding.) Next, who cares how many times someone tells you no, you don't give up.

J. K. Rowlings wrote *Harry Potter* and got more than a dozen rejection letters. The manuscript got tossed around, and finally a smart agent found it in a discard bin and thought it was good. She got $6,000 for that first manuscript. Eight books later, J. K. Rowlings is the most successful and highest-grossing author of all time. She didn't give up.

A little book called *The Shack* came out in 2007. It was about a man who had an incredible loss and in his grief discovered God. The authors made the rounds to twenty different publishers. The Christian publishers all rejected it because the subject matter was a bit too edgy for them. The mainstream publishers all rejected it because there was too much "Jesus" in the book.

Did the authors quit? No! They went to a local printer, printed up ten thousand copies, and sold it on their website. They sold out in three months. In one year, they sold a million books out of their garage.

My publishing house was started that way. I got tired of publishers telling me, "Black kids don't read," or, "No one will buy that," when I submitted proposals for books that weren't with a celebrity or had a salacious subject matter.

So instead of complaining and whining, picketing and creating a buzz, I said to myself, "I'm going to start my own publishing house and publish what I want to publish."

I can't expect a publisher who doesn't share my vision or experience to understand the need to put certain books into the marketplace, nor could I blame them.

I've had many discussions with white people over the need for affirmative action even in a post-Obama world. If left to their own devices, people are more inclined to hire people whom they are comfortable with, people who look like them, people who share their background.

What does that mean? White people would prefer to hire white people in their companies. How many blacks or whites do you see working in a Chinese restaurant? It's not necessarily racist. I don't see many whites working at *Black Enterprise* or *Ebony*. It's just the way it is.

So what do you do in the absence of affirmative

action—which may very well be on its way out for real?
You don't depend on anyone. You start your own business.

I think it's a shame that there are fewer black-
owned businesses in America than we had before the
Civil Rights Act was passed. Consider this: In 1939,
nearly 30,000 African-Americans owned retail outlets
and restaurants that employed more than 43,000 black
Americans and generated $71 million in sales. We had
more businesses during segregation and Jim Crow than
today? That's crazy, but it's true. And it has made us a
dependent group. We aren't self-sufficient.

We spend more than $700 billion as a nation, but
those dollars are not circulated back into our communities because we don't own anything. For everything we
need—from food, to clothing, to shelter—we must give
our money to some other group.

Maggie Lena Walker, whose mother was a former
slave and father an Irish abolitionist, had a vision of
starting a bank. In 1903, she founded and served as
president of St. Luke Penny Savings Bank—becoming
the first woman and first black to do so—with opening
day receipts of $9,430.44.

"Let us put our money together; let us use our

money; let us put our money out at usury among ourselves, and reap the benefits ourselves," she said.

Again, I learned firsthand watching my dad. He had a state job as a parole officer, but he ran his store, too.

"You will never become a millionaire working for somebody else," he would tell me. That stuck with me. It was true then and it's true today.

It's no coincidence that the first self-made black millionaire in this country—Madam C. J. Walker—made her millions running her own business. She went from washing white people's clothes for the first forty-plus years of her life, barely scraping by, to becoming a millionaire in less than five years. That was during the Great Depression!

So there can't be any excuses today. Few of us are up against the kind of racism, sexism, or any other ism that Madam C. J. Walker was up against. Few of us have the lack of educational access that she had. Few of us had so few role models from which to draw from and look to. No, we have it all. So why aren't we doing more?

It's time to get up and make it happen.

THREE

The Negro Must Keep Himself, His Children and His Home Clean and Make the Surroundings in Which He Lives Comfortable and Attractive

BURROUGHS

He must learn to "run his community up"—not down. We can segregate by law, we integrate only by living. Civilization is not a matter of race, it is a matter of standards. Believe it or not—someday, some race is going to outdo the Anglo-Saxon, completely. It can be the Negro race, if the Negro gets sense enough. Civilization goes up and down that way.

HUNTER

How prophetic. Living a good life has little to do with money. It has everything to do with accepting your condition or not accepting lower standards. I lived in a condo for seven years. A cleaning person would come in once a week to sweep and mop and vacuum the hallways and clean up around the building. On the days before the cleaner would come, litter would be around the building and even inside from time to time.

Guess what? I would get a broom and a dustpan and sweep up. Why? Because I lived there, and if I left the litter, it would pile up and make the home that I paid taxes on look like a pigsty. If someone dropped something inside the building, I would pick it up. While I didn't drop it, I didn't want to look at litter and debris.

The attitude of most of the people in my building was that they were paying a maintenance fee and shouldn't therefore have to pitch in extra to make sure their building looked clean. So they would rather see the litter pile up than lift one finger to improve the conditions. They had low standards.

Now, if this kind of attitude is prevalent in a decent neighborhood where people own their places, imagine how people act in low-income places. *Some* people. *Certain* people.

I have been to projects in white neighborhoods. I have been to projects in Jewish neighborhoods. And I have been to the projects of Chicago; Newark, New Jersey; Augusta, Georgia; and Harlem and Brooklyn, New York, where black people predominate. I will say without apology, the way many black people are living in the projects throughout the country is a sin and a crying shame. Graffiti on the walls, urine in the elevators and stairwells, drug dealers commandeering some of the common areas. It's crazy. There is no excuse for it. If the Jewish projects and the projects inhabited predominately by white people are neat and clean and don't even look like a project, why should black folks accept living like animals?

Yes, you can argue that perhaps the maintenance folks in the Jewish and white projects are doing their job better than those working in the black building. But even if that were the case, so what? That's about as ridiculous an argument as saying that because the books in the black schools in the 1950s were inferior, the blacks should simply not have gone to school. To hell with learning!

Well, whom are you hurting?

It's self-destructive and counterproductive to accept low living conditions.

I didn't think twice about cleaning up around my building. That's the way I was raised.

Donald Hunter, my father, who grew up in the heart of Newark, living among rats and roaches, refused to live that way when he had a choice. He was a strong advocate for what Ms. Burroughs expresses in this chapter.

When we moved into our neighborhood in the mid-1970s, the block was mixed. It slowly became an all-black neighborhood. But my father refused to allow the standards to dip, not one iota. In fact, the standards actually increased. Why? Because my father challenged our neighbors to step up their game. He would be out there in the fall, making sure our yard was leaf-free. In the spring and summer, he would be working in the yard with my mom, planting beautiful flowers, trimming the azalea bushes, and grooming the grass. He set the tone and the neighbors followed. It became a competition after a while to see who could have the greenest grass or plant the prettiest flowers.

High standards can be contagious, but it doesn't

necessarily happen through osmosis. Sometimes you have to budge people into doing the right thing—either by example or in a more obvious way.

When I used to sweep up around my building, some of my neighbors started pitching in, too—either because they were embarrassed or out of a sense of responsibility. But I would also leave notes around the building reminding them that just because they paid a maintenance fee, it didn't mean that they should allow our home to look bad. We all had a responsibility, and all it took was a little time. If we all pitched in, it would take just a fraction of time to keep things looking good.

In my parents' neighborhood, my dad took it upon himself to be the Welcome Wagon of sorts. He would engage the new neighbors in discussion and subtly talk about the pride he had in the neighborhood. They would get the message.

In 2006, a family—which happened to be a white family—moved in on the corner of my parents' block. They were from New York and had apparently never experienced having to groom a yard. They never cut their grass. They allowed weeds to grow up and made the corner of my parents' block an eyesore. Donald Hunter walked down the street and knocked on this family's door. He asked them politely if he could cut their grass. He didn't yell and scream or get in their faces about their lack of neighborhood pride, he simply said, "We have a certain standard here on Lafayette, and if you would like me to cut your grass once a week, I would be more than happy to."

The man was embarrassed, and instead of allowing my dad to cut his grass, he asked to borrow the mower (the man didn't even have a mower). He quickly got with the program. While he doesn't have the best grass, it's no longer bringing down the block. Pride can be contagious, but sometimes we have to help others get it. We have to hold one another accountable.

If everybody had that attitude, how much better would life be for everyone?

I know when I look good, I feel good. I know when I come home and my house is in order, everything else seems to fall into place for me. Shouldn't we strive for that all of the time?

FOUR

The Negro Must Learn to Dress More Appropriately for Work and for Leisure

BURROUGHS

Knowing what to wear—how to wear it—when to wear it and where to wear it, are earmarks of common sense, culture and also an index to character.

HUNTER

This rule of Burroughs's relates to chapter 3, but it's more personal. In the previous chapter, she is talking about our neighborhoods and how we are perceived as a community, in terms of our civilization and what we accept and expect as a community.

Here, she is talking about our personhood. What Burroughs is saying is that there is a time and a place for everything, and far too many of us don't know that. We wear our nightclub outfits to the office and our formal wear to church. In that way, what she's saying totally relates to the previous chapter in that just as people judge you by how you allow yourself to live, they also judge you by how you carry yourself personally. But more to the point, people judge your entire community by how *you* carry yourself.

I believe what she is saying goes beyond clothing. It's not what you wear, it's how you wear—your clothes, your attitude, your self-respect.

I have been known to tell a young man on the streets to pull up his pants. Why? Because that young man represents me in some way and I feel that I have a responsibility to him. Maybe he doesn't know that it's inappropriate to have your entire behind out and your underwear outside your pants. There was a time when you didn't have to tell a young black man something like that. We aren't living in those times anymore. Whatever Burroughs was dealing with in the 1890s and early 1900s pales in comparison to the level of inappropriate dress we have to endure today. But it must have been an issue even then to prompt her to write about it.

Yes, it would seem like common sense not to wear a negligee under your jacket to work. It would seem like common sense not to wear pants so tight that your moose knuckles show. It would seem so, but it's not.

Once again, we have a responsibility to one another to educate those who don't know. Now, you have to be careful *how* you do that. I don't recommend you just go up to strangers and start wagging your finger at them, but there is a way to do it. And we should.

Before you start chastising others, however, start with yourself. Are you always presentable? Do you represent not just your race but yourself at the highest level?

I teach at Hunter College, and I make sure that I am neat and wear a suit jacket and am presentable when I'm teaching. Now most professors are sloppy. They wear old jeans, run-down, dirty sneakers, and they look a mess. But I can't do that. I am the only black female in my department, and I don't just represent me. I represent all black females and all blacks who might ever teach at a university.

My students aren't from my community. If I have two black students in a class per semester, that's a lot.

But it's important for nonblacks to see us blacks looking good and being excellent. We may be the only black people they ever come in contact with, so we have to show our best foot.

I have a friend who worked for a major pharmaceutical company. It was typical corporate America. She was the only black female in her department. The company employed few blacks, period. The one high-powered black woman, a doctor, weighed more than 250 pounds and dressed in ill-fitting suits and muumuulike skirts. She was brilliant, but sloppy. The few black administrative assistants didn't quite know how to dress and their hair was never right.

My buddy made it her business to show up to work every day looking like Diahann Carroll or Diana Ross in *Mahogany*. She made a standing appointment to have her hair done every Friday, she worked out three or four times a week, and she shopped at Brooks Brothers, Ralph Lauren, and Ann Taylor (the outlets, of course) for the finest, timeless pieces. She was by far the best-dressed woman in her office, and that was her mission.

"These people had a very distinct impression of

black women," she said. "It was the same old stereo-type—we were either ghetto or completely white-acting. I made it my business to be one hundred percent black and fly as hell. I spoke well, I dressed well, I looked great, but I never let them forget that I loved being black. I never let them get away with that 'You're different' BS. I would say, 'All of my friends dress like this. All of my friends act like this.' It was my goal to break down every single stereotype they had. It was a lot of work on my part. But it was worth it."

I'm not saying that we should carry the weight of the black world on our shoulders when we walk into the workplace, but we should have a standard of excellence and realize that when people are looking at us, they are really looking at all of black America. You will help someone shape and define his or her image of black women and black men by the way you carry yourself. You might be the one to change someone's perspective for the better.

Having standards isn't really for anyone else. You should want to have them for yourself.

A lot of people died so that I can do the things I am doing. A lot of people fought hard so that I could have the right to teach in a university and write and publish books. A lot of people endured much hardship, humiliation, suffering, and pain. The least I can do is be my best, live my best life, and treat myself and my surroundings with respect.

FIVE

The Negro Must Make His Religion an Everyday Practice and Not Just a Sunday-Go-to-Meeting Emotional Affair

HUNTER

Burroughs didn't have anything to add to that statement. It actually needed no explanation. But I'm going to comment on it anyway because of all of the twelve things, I believe this is the most important.

If you have no faith or religion nor a belief in God, then skip this chapter. But if you call yourself a person of faith, then be real about it.

I had to get really real about my faith in 2006, when I was challenged by what seemed like every atheist in the world.

I was invited to be a guest panelist on *Paula Zahn Now* on CNN. I had appeared on her show frequently, and on this night one of the topics was a family of atheists who lived in the Bible Belt. They were complaining about being "discriminated against" and harassed for their beliefs (or lack thereof). Upon reading the story, I had determined that while no one should be harassed for being an atheist (or for any reason), this harassment was avoidable because how would anyone know these people were atheists? I mean, unless you're wearing a sign or have a bumper sticker on your car or you're vocal about it, how would anyone know that you don't believe in God?

And if they do know, then you must be making it an issue. In the Bible Belt? So was this family looking to be antagonistic and create a platform? It seemed so.

On the show, I said that atheists should shut up. If their goal is truly just to live their lives unencumbered by religion and God and all that comes with it, cool. Do that. If they are at a sporting event where people are praying, all they have to do is not pray. Simple. There is no need to say, "Hey, wait a minute, you people! I don't believe in God and I'm offended that you all are praying!"

I also cracked a joke about atheists needing better PR and perhaps they were jealous because Hallmark had overlooked them. I said maybe if they had a greeting card, they might feel better. It was a bad joke, but I never expected the reaction I received in the minutes, hours, days, months . . . you get the point . . . that followed. (I'm still getting e-mail from atheists as far away as England and Australia who were offended by my comments.) A YouTube piece even juxtaposed my statements to Dr. Martin Luther King Jr.'s "I Have a Dream" speech. I mean, really.

What I said then (and what I still believe) is this: Being an atheist is not a civil rights issue. It's not like being black or a woman or an Orthodox Jew or Muslim. And I feel assaulted by Richard Dawkins and his minions, who want to ram Darwinism down our throats, and who successfully removed prayer and any form of intelligent design from schools (watch out, intelligent design is a dangerous concept).

I've had debates with Neil deGrasse Tyson, the chief astrophysicist at the Hayden Planetarium in New York. Yes, I can roll with the Big Bang and all of that, but what was the catalyst. If it was all just a random series of occurrences, then why is our world (when not being messed over by humans) in such perfect order? If there is no God and there is nothing after we're gone, then explain that basic scientific law that matter (which is you and me and all living things) can neither be created nor destroyed. In all of their logic, they leave out quite a bit explaining. And if you don't agree with them, then you're dumb. But I do digress.

What I'm saying is that the foundation of any religion is faith. You have to just believe, in spite of not having hard, physical, scientific knowledge, that which is seemingly unbelievable. And if you truly do believe in God, then don't be half-assed about it—go all the way because isn't He worth fighting for?

So here goes: I believe that the removal of prayer was America's undoing. If the Founding Fathers could write—*We hold these Truths to be self-evident, that all men are created equal, that they are endowed by their Creator with certain unalienable Rights, that among these are Life, Liberty, and the Pursuit of Happiness*— then it should still stand.

That said, I was under heavy scrutiny and attack for my views and my "religion" (which I call more spirituality than religion). A petition was circulated by professors at Hunter College to have my appointment revoked. Students were urged to boycott my classes. Three of my e-mail accounts were virtually shut down by the bombardment I received. (Note: I had been a columnist with the New York *Daily News* for several years and had hosted a morning show in New York City and had made many, many controversial statements, and I had never received the kind of hate mail that I got over this atheist flap.)

I realized that I must have struck a nerve. I also realized that this was war and I had to be really serious about which side I stood on. I couldn't talk about loving the Lord and believing in God. I had to live it because I now represented Him beyond my tiny world. It became increasingly more important that I studied that word, that I knew that word, but more important, that I lived that word.

Church for me is not about getting up and going to a building on Sunday, but an everyday reflection and fellowship with other believers and working on my relationship with God.

If I'm going to open my mouth about God, I should at least know Him, right?

Beyond that, however, this notion of "Sunday-go-to meeting" is something we as black folks have obviously been guilty of for more than one hundred years, according to Nannie Burroughs. We hide behind our religion and throw that "religious" cloak over people instead of holding each other and our pastors and spiritual leaders accountable to the tenants of the Bible we are supposed to uphold. We allow too much sinning in our churches. This is not judgment, it's truth. As a result, many of us and our ministries aren't blessed. And we wonder why.

You can't be singing about Lord, Lord, on Sunday and acting like the devil Monday through Saturday. It just simply doesn't work.

The Bible talks about serving two masters. It also talks about being lukewarm in your faith. "So because you are lukewarm, and neither hot nor cold, I will spit you out of My mouth." (Revelations 3:16)

I grew up in the church. I was baptized in a Baptist church when I was eleven and attended Catholic schools from grammar school throughout high school. My college, Drew University, is known for having one of the best theological seminaries in the nation. I spent a lot of time talking to ministers, priests, and rabbis, and I've concluded that most people, a vast majority of people, are fakers and shakers when it comes to serving their God.

Sure, they may be able to quote Scripture. They can clutch their Bibles and Torahs and Korans and put on the face of piety, but few people actually live the truth of their faith.

What Burroughs is expressing in this chapter is deep. What she is saying is that your religion, your faith, your beliefs, have to be lived out every single day—not just on Saturday or Sunday, or whatever day is prescribed by your religion for meeting. It's not for you to go to church or mosque or temple and have the religious leader preach to you and read some Scriptures, but it's work that you must put in yourselves the other six days as well.

Your faith should not be a passive activity in your life.

If you want a relationship with God, it must be a two-way street. You can't say you love God and make no moves to get to know His character, His desires and vision for your life.

You cannot profess to be a person of faith and have no manifestation of that faith in your life. Just as *love* is a verb, so is *faith*.

I know there is a God because there is evidence. Great pediatric neurosurgeon Ben Carson believes there is a God and talks about it often. Even in his vast scientific mind, he sees the hand of God. What made Charles Drew decide that blood could be separated and stored? How is it that a square inch of muscle is stronger than a piece of steel? Did that happen by accident? That was some random selection, some evolutionary process?

God has given us free will right down to our cells. They can create a bladder: by laying bladder cells on top of a mold of a bladder, that will form into a perfectly healthy bladder that can be transplanted into a body.

Intelligent design? No, God. I'm sold-out and definitive about it.

Scientist George Washington Carver had a great story about his relationship with God. One time, he cried to the Lord, "Oh, Mr. Creator, why did You make the universe?" To which God replied, "You want to know too much for that little mind of yours. Ask me something more your size."

So Carver responded, "Dear Mr. Creator, tell me what man was made for."

Still too big. Finally he asked, "Mr. Creator, why did You make the peanut?"

Carver went on to invent more than three hundred uses for the peanut.

What is your purpose? Why are you here? Start small and find out.

SIX

The Negro Must Highly Resolve to Wipe Out Mass Ignorance

BURROUGHS

The leaders of the race must teach and inspire the masses to become eager and determined to improve mentally, morally and spiritually, and to meet the basic requirements of good citizenship.

We should initiate an intensive literacy campaign in America, as well as in Africa. Ignorance—satisfied ignorance—is a millstone about the neck of the race. It is democracy's greatest burden.

Social integration is a relationship attained as a result of the cultivation of kindred social ideals, interests and standards. It is a blending process that requires time, understanding and kindred purposes to achieve. Likes alone, and not laws can do it.

HUNTER

Malcolm X went into jail as Malcolm Little, a hustler, cocaine addict, and burglar. He left jail a man of enormous vision, power, and wisdom. He began by reading and memorizing words in the dictionary because he had so little education that he was unable to read the most simple of books and couldn't construct a proper letter. This awakened a thirst in him to want to know more. Once he mastered words, he began to read everything he could get his hands on. He would even sneak and read after lights-out at 10 p.m. every night by the glow of the light in the landing of his cellblock.

"Ten guards and the warden couldn't have torn me out of those books," he said. "I have often reflected upon the new vistas that reading opened to me. I knew right there in prison that reading had changed forever the course of my life."

Reading, knowledge, learning, are the gateways to power and excellence.

Here's the deal. When a nation attempts to conquer

or take over another nation, the first thing it does is destroy the books and kill the scribes (the writers) and the teachers. Why? Because if people have access to knowledge, all things are possible.

There is a reason why slaves were forbidden to read under threat of death. Knowledge opens the path to the impossible. If you can perceive something, you can achieve it. The slave masters knew if a slave learned to read, he would learn to think. If he learned to think, he would start to know. Once he gained knowledge, it would be just a matter of time before he figured out the truth—that he *wasn't* inferior, that he wasn't an animal or three-fifths a man, and that he was worthy of freedom. Once that genie got out of the bottle, it would be a wrap.

So they beat and killed any slave that was found to know how to read or who was responsible for teaching another.

My question: Why is it that a people that should know more than any other group about the power and importance of reading and education allow the public schools to do such a lousy job educating their children? Why do we allow our children's reading scores to be so low and so far behind every other group? Why don't we push and promote and support authors who are writing real literature, producing provocative books, and uncovering and reporting truths?

If this book doesn't sell a million copies, I want to know why. And not for me. But Nannie Helen Burroughs deserves to be a household name in every black home in America, and her words of wisdom must be handed down so that we don't go another hundred years and these points are still relevant. Yes, I'm repeating that last point because it must be repeated.

People died so that we could have access, yet many of us still don't have a computer, and those of us who do have one use it to hook up on Internet dating sites, and games sites, and MySpace, and Facebook, not to educate ourselves.

We can't complain about what the school system hasn't done when we have access to all of the knowledge in the world. It's all in a book. When was the last time you read something to feed your mind?

I see a correlation to the rampant obesity in our community with our lack of a desire to gobble up knowledge. They say you are what you eat. Well, many of us eat McDonald's and a bunch of other fast foods. It feeds our hunger, but it doesn't nourish our bodies.

In fact, it makes us unhealthy and fat. We're no longer hungry, but that food is killing us. (Check out *SuperSize Me*, the Morgan Spurlock documentary.)

The things we put into our minds follow the same arc. Every time you read a book about a hustler or a drug dealer or some sad story about how a woman was done wrong by her man, every time you read a cheap thriller and you don't balance your diet with a little history, a little spiritual reading, perhaps even a well-done childrens' book, you are making your mind unhealthy.

Just as you are what you eat, you are also what you read.

If all you read is crap, so will your mind be crap. Balance. But more important, read things that matter. It's okay to read a fun, titillating book from time to time. But that can't be the only thing you read. If that's all you're reading, you don't have much knowledge to share with anyone else.

That's why we're here, I believe, to not just take for our own lives, but to impart things to others as a blessing to them.

So the more you know, the more you can show and help others to grow.

SEVEN

The Negro Must Stop Charging His Failures Up to His "Color" and to White Peoples' Attitudes

BURROUGHS

The truth of the matter is that good service and conduct will make senseless race prejudice fade like mist before the rising sun. God never intended that a man's color shall be anything other than a badge of distinction.

It is high time that all races were learning that fact. The Negro must first QUALIFY for whatever position he wants. Purpose, initiative, ingenuity and industry are the keys that all men use to get what they want. The Negro will have to do the same. He must make himself a workman who is too skilled not to be wanted, and too DEPENDABLE not to be on the job, according to promise or plan. He will never become a vital factor in industry until he learns to put into his work the vitalizing force of initiative, skill and dependability.

He has gone "RIGHTS" mad and "DUTY" dumb.

HUNTER

Rights mad and duty dumb. Keep in mind, Burroughs wrote this before there was ever a March on Washington or before a single civil rights law was passed. She wrote this in a time just after reconstruction when blacks were trying to figure out their role in America. While it was a time that would surely inspire many to want all of the rights that had been denied them for over two hundred years, Burroughs said, "Earn it!"

For some, this seemed like an Uncle Tom (or Aunt Thomasina) stance. But I get it. She's right. You can't expect people to do the right thing just because it's the right thing to do. The majority of the time, if left to their own devices, people *won't* do the right things by others.

So what do you do? Jump up and down and scream and complain about it? No, you roll up your sleeves and work. Back then, I can't imagine what it must have been like because people did put one foot in front of the other and worked their behinds off.

Today, however, we are a nation of slackers—black and white and other. We are a nation that rewards and applauds mediocrity. We are a nation of people who say things like "Well, at least I'm not as bad as that guy!" But what happened to being the best?

Once, *Made in America* meant something. When people had pride in their abilities. Once, you didn't get knocked for being good or excellent.

Today, a kid gets ridiculed for being too smart. Why? Because others are mediocre and they don't want the smart kid showing them up or raising the bar so that now the mediocre ones have to work a little harder.

I ended up at the New York *Daily News* on some affirmative-action stuff, and I am a strong advocate for affirmative action. However . . .

I have no problem with your getting into the door just because you are black, even if your scores or your credentials don't match a white person's. Systemic racism is real, and it's not a level playing field, so let's not pretend. But once you get in the door, you better work your behind off to not just slip by, but to excel.

That's what I was committed to doing.

When I first got to the *News,* I worked in the high school sports department. My direct superior at the time couldn't wait to tell me, "You know, you're only here because you're black. This slot had to be filled by a black person."

It was on. "Oh, really," I said to him. But I was thinking, "Well, I'm going to show you how a black person gets down."

I hustled, and the following week I offered a sports story to the Sunday section, and it ended up on the front page of the Sunday section of the *News*—the highest circulating edition of the week.

One of my coworkers said to me, "I've been here eleven years and I've never had a front-page story."

I said to her, "I guess you have to work a little harder."

Yeah, I could have been more humble about it. But I was young and they were trying to make me feel as if I didn't belong there and that I was just some affirmative-action hire. I needed to prove that while affirmative action got me in the door, my hard work and talent would get me a key made.

Over the next few years, I graduated to cover crime on the city side—a move not many sportswriters were able to make. I covered business, wrote features, and in 1994, I was invited to sit on the prestigious editorial board. They already had a black person on the board, so it wasn't for affirmative-action reasons.

My editor, Michael Goodwin, told me that he was looking for someone with strong opinions who could write about a range of subjects, and my skills more than qualified me for the position. I had never written an editorial in my life and didn't know if I could do it. But I had prepared for it. I was given education—the biggest beat on the board, and wrote pieces that changed school governance laws in the State of New York. I also covered child welfare. In 1999, I participated in a series of editorials to save the world-famous Apollo Theatre, for which our editorial board won the Pulitzer Prize.

That's what happens when you commit yourself to not just being there, not just doing enough to get by, but working to be the best.

If you're going to be the only black in a position, let them remember you were there—for good reasons.

After the Pulitzer, I became the first black woman ever to write a news column for the *News*. These things were not handed to me. I had some great editors and some great support, but I also worked hard to be successful with no excuses.

EIGHT

The Negro Must Overcome His Bad Job Habits

BURROUGHS

He must make a brand new reputation for himself in the world of labor. His bad job habits are absenteeism, funerals to attend, or a little business to look after. The Negro runs an off and on business. He also has a bad reputation for conduct on the job—such as, petty quarrelling with other help, incessant loud talking about nothing; loafing, carelessness, due to lack of job pride; insolence, gum chewing and—too often—liquor drinking. Just plain bad job habits!

HUNTER

So people were lying about a dead grandmother a hundred years ago to get out of work? Wow.

Today, people come to work and sit surfing the Web, sending personal e-mails, and making personal phone calls. That's stealing. That's being niggardly. If you're sitting around your office spreading gossip, backstabbing, and creating dissension, you are being niggardly—with not just your job, but with yourself. You aren't creating an environment where you will excel, and worse, you are making it a bad work environment for those around you.

Yet, that seems to be more the norm in offices across the country.

People show up late, they leave early, they take longer-than-allowed lunches, then wonder why they aren't promoted or why they get written up or fired. Unfortunately, most people don't accept responsibility when these things happen. They will blame the boss, they will blame a coworker, they will blame their spouse or even their kids. But the problem is in the mirror.

In Matthew 25:13-30, Jesus warns us about slacking and thinking we're getting away with something:

Therefore stay alert, because you do not know the day or the hour. For it is like a man going on a journey, who summoned his slaves and entrusted his property to them. To one he gave five talents, to another two, and to another one, each according to his ability. Then he went on his journey. The one who had received five talents went off right away and put his money to work and gained five more. In the same way, the one who had two gained two more. But the one who had received one talent went out and dug a hole in the ground and hid his master's money in it.

After a long time, the master of those slaves came and settled his accounts with them. The one who had received the five talents came and brought five more, saying, "Sir, you entrusted me with five talents. See, I have gained five more." His master answered, "Well done, good and faithful slave! You have been faithful in a few things. I will put you in charge of many things. Enter into the joy of your master." The one with the two talents also came and said, "Sir, you entrusted two talents to me. See, I have gained two more."

His master answered, "Well done, good and faithful slave! You have been faithful with a few things. I will put you in charge of many things. Enter into the joy of your master."

Then the one who had received the one talent came and said, "Sir, I knew that you were a hard man, harvesting where you did not sow, and gathering where you did not scatter seed, so I was afraid, and I went and hid your talent in the ground. See, you have what is yours." But his master answered, "Evil and lazy slave! So you knew that I harvest where I didn't sow and gather where I didn't scatter? Then you should have deposited my money with the bankers, and on my return I would have received my money back with interest!

"Therefore take the talent from him and give it to the one who has ten. For the one who has will be given more, and he will have more than enough. But the one who does not have, even what he has will be taken from him. And throw that worthless slave into the outer darkness, where there will be weeping and gnashing of the teeth."

Jesus was making a comparison to how we handle the gifts we have been given here on earth. In the case of these slaves the metaphor is salvation, and those who took the opportunity to be saved and ran with it and didn't squander it got more. But the one who buried it and wasted it ended up gnashing his teeth.

Even if you think you're getting away with being a slacker on your job or, worse, disruptive and a menace, it will eventually catch up to you. You will certainly pay the consequences.

And don't think that just because some other workers around you are worse than you, that will somehow save you. It would seem fair, but life isn't fair. Your only saving grace is to do what you're supposed to do and not worry about what the next person is doing. You do the right thing.

One editor at the *Daily News* had a drinking problem. Everyone knew it. He would show up to work drunk, looking disheveled and a mess. He got away with it and kept his nice six-figure job . . . for a while. Somewhere inside, I knew I could never get away with that (not that I ever wanted to). But I knew that just because he could do it didn't mean that I could get away with anything.

I was once told that I could never get fired because someone in my department had referred to me as a nigger and wasn't fired.

"You can always point to that," I was told.

I never wanted to test that one because as much as it seemed that would be a great defense, I would rather stay on my job because I was good at what I did. I would rather be good than to be there because someone else, who referred to me as a nigger, got to keep his job.

In 2004, I filed my last piece for the *Daily News*. I wrote a column about a man who had given perhaps the best speech at a presidential convention I had ever heard. In this column, I talked about how the country needed to hear more from this man because he understood what America is supposed to be about. That man was Barack Obama.

I was an editorial columnist for the *Daily News* at the time, and I decided that the kind of work I was now being asked to do was beneath my talents. I had a new editor with whom I had history and it wasn't good. I decided to not stay in a situation that would compromise my ethics, where I could have kept the job by complying.

Instead of staying and being sour and disruptive, instead of turning in mediocre work out of defense and rebellion, I left because it's better to leave a job on a high note, on your own terms, than to stay with a bad reputation or be asked to leave.

NINE

The Negro Must Improve His Conduct in Public Places

BURROUGHS

Taken as a whole, he is entirely too loud and too ill-mannered. There is much talk about wiping out racial segregation and also much talk about achieving integration.

Segregation is a physical arrangement by which people are separated in various services. It is definitely up to the Negro to wipe out the apparent justification or excuse for segregation.

The only effective way to do it is to clean up and keep clean. By practice, cleanliness will become a habit and habit becomes character.

HUNTER

This is a common theme and one that Burroughs has hit on before. She talks about behavior on the job, keeping the neighborhood clean, keeping the kids disciplined, keeping yourself presentable. This is an extension of that. So no need to labor the point.

Stop acting ignorant in public (and private, too, for that matter!).

TEN

The Negro Must Learn How to Operate Business for People— Not for Negro People, Only

BURROUGHS

To do business, [the Negro] will have to remove all typical "earmarks," business principles; measure up to accepted standards and meet stimulating competition, graciously—in fact, he must learn to welcome competition.

HUNTER

I have a friend who owns a business and is constantly complaining about how black people don't support her business. Well, her storefront is dirty, her food is inconsistent in quality, and her customer service is horrible. Why should black people support her business? Simply because she's black?

When spending your dollars, you should demand the best. Those who own businesses must make sure that their business is up to par. You can't expect black people—or any people—to support your business just because you share the same race. That's ludicrous.

Why should we even know that a business is owned by a black person? You shouldn't! I learned this from the master firsthand. As I mentioned, my dad owned a corner store in the heart of Newark, New Jersey, on Ridgewood and Madison avenues. My father was not what you would call a domesticated man. I don't think he ever changed a diaper, and not until he was into his sixties did he even attempt to cook a meal—and that was breakfast, the easiest meal in the world to fix. But every evening when he got home from closing the store, he would wash the lab coats that his employees were required to wear.

My dad believed that crisp, white lab coats sent a message to his patrons. He sold fruits and vegetables and everyday items. If you needed it, he sold it, and he demanded that his workers be polite and wear those lab coats. He hired youth from the neighborhood, but he trained them.

His corner store was better than the local grocery store. Even Shaquille O'Neal, when he was in high school, and a few others would stop into Hunter's Corner Store in Newark.

When I started my publishing house, my goal was that it not be a *black* publishing house. But rather that it would be a *major* publishing house. While I didn't have the resources of a major house, I wanted my books and my authors to be on par with any at the mainstream houses (no, I'm lying, I wanted them to be better).

Do what you do, but do it excellently.

How many times have you walked into a business in the hood and they cash your check, you can pay your gas and electricity bill, buy a T-shirt, grab a sandwich, and get the latest bootleg DVD all in the same place? What the heck is that? They may be making money, but they aren't running a good business.

How many times have you been to a black take-out restaurant and the fried fish isn't quite fresh, the macaroni and cheese is not hot and cheesy, and the place isn't quite clean? Why do you keep going back?

We live in a capitalist society. Supply and demand is

the lay of the land. While I would prefer to spend my dollars in my community, that establishment has to be worthy of my money just as much as any other business.

Just as we should support our businesses, those in business should work extra hard to make sure that not only blacks but everyone will want to spend money with them.

ELEVEN

The Average So-Called Educated
Negro Will Have to Come Down out
of the Air. He Is Too Inflated Over
Nothing. He Needs an Experience
Similar to the One That Ezekiel
Had—(Ezekiel 3:14-19). And
He Must Do What Ezekiel Did.
Otherwise, Through Indifference, as
to the Plight of the Masses, the Negro,
Who Thinks That He Has Escaped,
Will Lose His Own Soul

BURROUGHS

It will do all leaders good to read Hebrews 13:3, and the
first thirty-seven chapters of Ezekiel. A race transforms

itself through its own leaders and its sensible "common people." A race rises on its own wings, or is held down by its own weight.

True leaders are never "things apart from the people." They are the masses. They simply got to the front ahead of them. Their only business at the front is to inspire the masses by hard work and noble example and challenge them to "Come on!"

Dante stated a fact when he said, "Show the people the light and they will find the way!"

There must arise within the Negro race a leadership that is not out hunting bargains for itself. A noble example is found in the men and women of the Negro race, who, in the early days, laid down their lives for the people. Their invaluable contributions have not been appraised by the "latter-day leaders."

In many cases, their names would never be recorded, among the unsung heroes of the world, but for the fact that white friends have written them there.

"Lord, God of Hosts, be with us yet."

The Negro of today does not realize that, but, for these exhibits A's, that certainly show the innate possibilities of members of their own race, white people would not have been moved to make such princely investments in lives and money, as they have made, for the establishment of schools and for the on-going of the race.

HUNTER

There must have been a bunch of bourgeois, saddity black folks during Burroughs's time because she spoke the longest about this subject. And the message: Stop thinking more of yourself than you ought. Just because you have been blessed with position, money, or great intellect doesn't make you better than anyone else. The Bible says to whom much is given, much is required. That means if you have much, it is your responsibility to share it with others. You must become a servant to others.

Jesus washed the feet of his disciples to show that a man who was the most spiritual and godly (the son of God!) could humble himself (and imagine how dirty those feet must have been back then).

If Jesus can do that, then who are we? Who do we think we are?

If you are blessed with physical beauty, know that it is a blessing. You didn't do anything to be beautiful (and don't think that the plastic surgery you had makes you more beautiful). If you've been blessed with a high IQ, please know that it is a blessing. You must have been given that intellect for a reason; use it to teach and help others learn and grow. It's not just for you to show off and make people around you feel stupid.

If you've been blessed with money and position, know that it is a blessing. While you may have worked your fanny off to obtain the dough and the power, know that it is by the grace of God that you have any of it, and you were given the drive, determination, moxie, and talents to get it all for a reason. It's not just for you to use as a weapon against others or to show people up.

It's a blessing.

I have been in a position to know quite a few wealthy and talented people. Few of them seem to get this. They are under the impression that their wealth, fame, position, and power are all for them. That it's all about them.

It's ugly to watch people mistreat people because they feel that their money, fame, or power entitles them to speak to people any kind of way or to treat folks dismissively.

They are wrong.

The Negro Must Stop Forgetting His Friends. Remember!

BURROUGHS

Read Deuteronomy 24:18. Deuteronomy rings the big bell of gratitude. Why? Because an ingrate is an abomination in the sight of God. God is constantly telling us that "I, the Lord thy God delivered you"—through human instrumentalities.

The American Negro has had and still has friends—in the North and in the South. These friends not only pray, speak, write, influence others, but make unbelievable, unpublished sacrifices and contributions for the advancement of the race—for their brothers in bonds. The noblest thing that the Negro can do is to so live and labor that these benefactors will not have given in vain. The Negro must make his heart warm with gratitude, his lips sweet with thanks and his heart and mind resolute with purpose to justify the sacrifices and stand on his feet and go forward—"God is no respector of persons. In every nation, he that feareth him and worketh righteousness is" sure to win out. Get to work! That's the answer to everything that hurts us. We talk too much about nothing instead of redeeming the time by working.

R-E-M-E-M-B-E-R

In spite of race prejudice, America is brim full of opportunities. Go after them!

HUNTER

A friend of mind, Grammy winner Teddy Vann, said to me during one of the first times we met, "Always honor the introduction." I didn't quite understand what he meant then, but today I do.

No matter where you are in life, someone gave you a leg up, or an introduction. Never forget that person. Never forget where you came from and how you got there.

I don't have many friends, but I am blessed to have

the ones that I do. I don't toss that word *friend* around loosely. I believe that a friend, a true friend, has to pass certain tests.

What Burroughs is saying is even broader. When she talks about friends, she's really talking about legacy. When people such as Oprah and Tyler Perry talk of the giants upon whose shoulders they stand, that's what Burroughs is talking about. Don't forget that someone opened the doors before you.

Before there was a Sidney Poitier, there was a Paul Robeson getting his behind handed to him by white America. Before there was a Janet Jackson, there was an Eartha Kitt being run out of the country for being bold enough to speak her mind. Before there was a Jamie Foxx or Chris Rock, there was a Pigmeat Markum who had to endure unthinkable humiliation to even work as a comedian. Before there was an Usher or even a Michael Jackson, there was a Bill "Bojangles" Robinson. And before any of those people, there were slaves with gifts and talents we may never know about who lived and overcame so that we could be here today.

Before there was a Tyler Perry there was a Melvin Van Peebles and a Gordon Parks and a Flip Wilson.

Before there was an Earl Graves or a Bob Johnson,

there was a Madam C. J. Walker and a Mary Lena Walker.

Before there was an Oprah Winfrey, there was a Bev Smith and a Sue Simmons and a Jane Kennedy—there were people who banged on and cracked that door that made it possible for her to walk through it.

Before there was a Tiger Woods and a Venus and Serena, there was an Althea, and an Arthur, a Lee Elder and a Charlie Sifford and countless other nameless black folks who while they weren't allowed to play golf and tennis alongside whites were just as good as them, if not better, and never gave up their dream.

Before there was a Barack Obama, there was a Barbara Jordan, a Martin, a Malcolm, a Medgar, an Adam, a Thurgood, a Shirley Chisholm. There was a Fannie Lou Hamer who was "sick and tired of being sick and tired." And before there was a Marva Collins or a Karen Hunter, there was a Nannie Helen Burroughs.

Somebody came before you and made it possible.

Remember that!